THE **ADLARD COLES** BOOK OF

MEDITERRANEAN CRUISING

THIRD EDITION

ROD HEIKELL

ADLARD COLES NAUTICAL
LONDON

Acknowledgements

Special thanks to my wife Lu who crews, edits, comments gently and who took many of the photos. Also Anton Stanwix for suggestions and help, Murray Pereira for a wider view of the Mediterranean, Grum Sabat for laid-back suggestions, and all those people on small boats with generous spirits who make it such a wonderful life. Thanks to Willie Wilson and Nigel Patten for photos. Thanks to the RYA for checking over technical details and to the CA for information. At Adlard Coles Nautical Jessica Cole diligently edited this book and Janet Murphy organised it all and was patient over the timescale.

Published by Adlard Coles Nautical
an imprint of Bloomsbury Publishing Plc
50 Bedford Square,
London WC1B 3DP
www.adlardcoles.com

Copyright © Rod Heikell 2004, 2008, 2012

All photos Rod and Lu Heikell except
where stated.

First edition published as *The RYA Book of Mediterranean Cruising* 2004
Second edition published as *The Adlard Coles Book of Mediterranean Cruising* 2008
Third edition 2012

ISBN: 978-1-4081-5283-6
ePub ISBN: 978-1-4081-5916-3
ePDF ISBN: 978-1-4081-4634-7

The right of the author to be identified as the author of this work has been asserted by him in accordance with the Copyright, Designs and Patents Act, 1988.

A CIP catalogue record for this book is available from the British Library.

This book is produced using paper that is made from wood grown in managed, sustainable forests. It is natural, renewable and recyclable. The logging and manufacturing processes conform to the environmental regulations of the country of origin. Typeset in 11 on 12.5pt Sabon
Printed in China by C&C Offset Printing Co., Ltd., Shenzhen, Guangdong.

Note: while all reasonable care has been taken in the publication of this book, the publisher takes no responsibility for the use of the methods or products described in the book.

Contents

Preface

Sailing to the Mediterranean Sea was once akin to the Grand Adventure. But now that we holiday in all sorts of exotic locations, it has become more familiar. We cook and eat Italian and French food. We go on charter sailing holidays to Greece and Croatia. But despite this apparent familiarity, this inland sea still draws people back like no other in the world.

For me the wonder of the Med is that you can sail across a relatively short bit of sea and straightaway you are in a country that is totally different from the one you left. The language, the cuisine, the cultural fabric are all unique and the people are evidently Spanish or French or Greek or Turkish. And despite worries that the grand project of the EU would homogenise the different cultures it encompassed, it seems that, to the contrary, the member countries have taken care to preserve their cultural and national identities. Where else can you cruise where there are so many different countries in so few miles of water?

All sorts of stereotypes abound about sailing in the Mediterranean and I hope that I dispel a few in this book. It can be windy, on average more so than northern European waters. It has short vicious seas that will stop you in your tracks. It is no more overcrowded than many other places and less so than many popular cruising areas such as the south coast of England.

It probably has less paperwork than in the UK and Mediterranean officials have a wonderful capacity for waving red tape away and ignoring silly regulations from Brussels. An increasing number of people now base their boat permanently in the Mediterranean and fly out on low fare airlines or on charter flights, to use the boat for anything from a few days to a few months. Apart from the fact that it can cost less to berth a boat in the Med, it can be remarkably cheap to fly out to the boat.

If there is one thing I'd like to stress it is that the desire to sail on this huge inland sea is more important than the boat, the equipment, or even finances. The first yacht I sailed from the UK to the Med many years ago was 20 feet long with an engine that defied any notions the word 'temperamental' might mean. All sorts of people are still sailing there on many types of boat; one of my pleasures is meeting new sailing folk, going for sundowners, sailing in company for a bit, sharing a few meals and establishing a special kind of camaraderie. You have no idea who that person is on the other boat in the anchorage. All you know is that he has invited you over for a drink to watch a Mediterranean sunset and that's a good enough recommendation for me.

Rod Heikell

1 The Mediterranean Sea

To make sense of the Mediterranean you need to turn the concept of ocean cruising inside out. The Pacific and the Atlantic are all about large tracts of water with some land around the edge and a few little dots of land scattered around the water. In the Mediterranean, the land defines the sea and you cannot sail in a straight line for very far without bumping into the stuff. The lands around occupy the sea and hence shape its character.

SOME FACTS ABOUT THE MED

- The Med is 2300 miles long, from Gibraltar to Iskenderun in southeast Turkey. At its widest, with a bit of a dog-leg, it is 1100 miles from Trieste at the top of the Adriatic to the Gulf of Sirte in Libya.
- The surface area is 1.46 million square miles. This is about 1/140th of the total sea area in the world. Its volume ranks only 1/355th in the world.
- Its mean depth is 1500 metres and its greatest depth (southwest of Cape Matapan in Greece) is 4600 metres – which is only slightly more than the mean depth of the Atlantic. Paradoxically, it seems deep to yachtsmen because depths drop off quickly from the land and you can often sail close to the coast in 50 metres of water.
- The Mediterranean is virtually tideless. At springs, the tidal difference at Gibraltar is 0.9 metres, at Gabes in Tunisia it is 1.8 metres, and at Khalkis in Greece it is 0.8 metres. But these are exceptions for the Mediterranean with most spring ranges around 0.1–0.2 metres so, for all intents and purposes, you can forget about tidal differences.
- Evaporation from the surface of the Mediterranean causes an annual loss of around 2900 cubic kilometres, about 1/1000th of the total volume. Rainfall and rivers replace around 1450 cubic kilometres. The rest flows in from the Atlantic, around 450,000 litres every second. It takes around 180 years for all the water in the Mediterranean to be renewed.
- The Mediterranean is tilted on a north to south axis so that the southern side is around 1 metre lower than the north side.
- Average wind strengths are higher in the Mediterranean than in northern Europe. For example, at four locations along the south coast of England, average wind speeds over the year are 8, 9, 9, 9 knots. At four locations along the south coast of France the annual average wind speeds are 11, 11, 9, 8 knots.
- The highest recorded wave in the Mediterranean is 12 metres, in the Sicilian Strait.

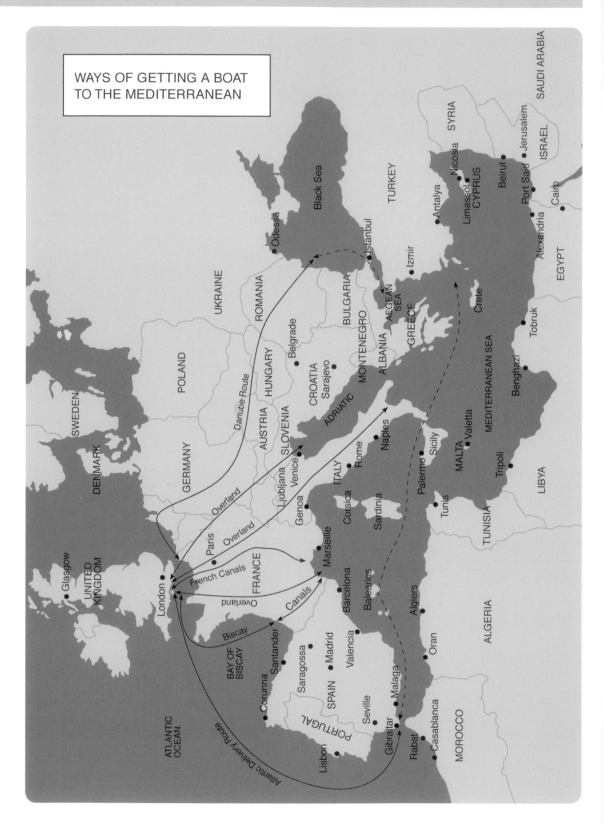

WAYS OF GETTING A BOAT
TO THE MEDITERRANEAN

In the Mediterranean, it is the land that is the defining feature rather than the vast tracts of water as with the Atlantic and Pacific Oceans.

The land and its history

The Mediterranean straddles the Occident and the Orient. If we take Italy as a dividing line, everything to the west is the Occident and to the east is the Orient. From this broad division between west and east, you can go back to the Mediterranean as a whole, but this time carve it into three civilisations: the Christian world, the Orthodox world and Islam. These divisions exist intact not only nowadays, but can be traced through the convoluted history of the Mediterranean from very early on. From this inland sea, the impact of the three civilisations stretches thousands of miles, across the oceans on either side and to the continents to the north and south.

The Christian world

The first of these civilisations is the western culture corresponding to the Occident. It is the Christian world, formerly the Roman Catholic world, with Rome at the hub. As such it spread north to split into the Protestant Church and its myriad offspring; from there Catholics and Protestants together migrated to the New World and colonised it. So much of the Protestant ethic of converting those in faraway lands to our western ideals

3

evolved from theological beliefs centred in Rome.

The Greek Orthodox Church

The second division is the Greek Orthodox world. Until quite recently, western historians paid only scant attention to Byzantium and its legacy; indeed few of us comprehend the current extent of the Orthodox Church, and fewer still its antecedents. From Greece, the Orthodox Church covers the Balkan peninsula, Bulgaria, Croatia, Serbia, Romania and north – up to the vastness of Russia. Until the Ottoman Turks overran it in 1453, the Orthodox Church (then the Holy Roman Empire in the east), the Byzantine Empire, had its centre at Constantinople. Since then Orthodoxy has been without a centre although not without power, as illustrated by the Cyprus troubles in the 1960s. Archbishop Makarios wanted Cyprus to be wholly part of the Greek Orthodox world; however, Islam and the Turkish Army eventually decided otherwise.

All over Greece you will find Orthodox churches and chapels reminding us of the schism long ago between Rome and Constantinople, and the dividing of the Christian world in the Mediterranean.

Islam

Islam is the third division of the Mediterranean, starting at Turkey on the eastern end of the Mediterranean and running around its southern shores to Morocco. It extends from there into Africa, across the Indian Ocean to Indonesia, the Philippines and the islands in the Melanesian archipelago. Islam has recently asserted itself with the new fundamentalism centred on Iran, Pakistan and Afghanistan; spreading from there to Lebanon and fomenting the bloody civil war between Muslim and Christian, and then to Palestine and farther west to Algeria. The effect of Islam on the Mediterranean was considerable when the Ottoman Empire held sway over all of Greece, the Balkans, and threatened Italy and Malta. From North Africa, the Arab invasions of Spain introduced Islam to Europe at the western end of the Mediterranean. The legacy of Islam was not just the obvious cultural influences as seen in cuisine, music and dress, but also on agriculture with the introduction of new species and methods of irrigation, in science and architecture; these influences spread throughout the Catholic and Orthodox worlds and remained after the Turks and Arabs left.

Cultural influences

The Mediterranean is one huge melting pot of these three major civilisations and when you sail around this inland sea you touch on all these cultural influences, both directly and indirectly. Sometimes the political boundary of a country conceals a great deal more than it reveals. Most of Aristotle and Socrates was preserved by Arab libraries while the books were destroyed in western monasteries. Salt cod is used in dishes throughout the Mediterranean although the cod arrives from Scandinavia and is not native to the Med. One of our most popular beverages, coffee, was just one of Islam's legacies to the west. Tomatoes and peppers, a mainstay of eastern dishes, were, however, brought by European explorers

Around the eastern Mediterranean, slender minarets pierce the sky as a reminder of the Islamic influence on Mediterranean culture.

One of my favourite cruising areas is the west coast of Italy between Naples and the Strait of Messina. This is Scario, situated along this stretch of coast.

from the Americas. The bougainvillaea you see everywhere in the Med is named after the French captain Bougainville, and comes from South America.

This huge history is one you should take some time to study, starting with a few potted histories followed by some more detailed books on the sea. It has a long history – possibly the longest – and certainly the longest in recorded history. The father of modern history, Herodotus, was born and taught in Halicarnassus, present day Bodrum in Turkey. But it is another more recent historian, Plotinus, who instructs us aptly that 'To any vision must be brought an eye adapted to what is to be seen'.

The ten most common questions I'm asked

Most of the answers to these questions are in this book, but I'll deal briefly with them and direct you elsewhere for a longer answer, if there is one.

1 Which cruising area is the best in the Mediterranean?

Apart from the obvious imputation of 'best', I'll stick with Plotinus and say that everyone has a different 'best' for different reasons.

As far as I am concerned, I count myself lucky to be able to visit so many countries in such close proximity and

It's getting harder all the time to find deserted anchorages but it is still possible. Kizil Burun in Turkey.

find such unexpected things there.

If there is one thing that annoys me it is those who become so obsessed with living cheaply that they lose out on the whole essence of experiencing another country. I don't have a lot of money, certainly less than many who are cruising in the Mediterranean, but if I hear one more conversation on how such-and-such is a great place because you can buy your beer at one pence less than up the road, I will scream. There is often a deafening silence about the beautiful scenery, the clear water, the smiley old man who runs the general store, the cheeky local bar owner and the wonderful goatherder's house perched on the edge of a cliff. I didn't sail all this distance to save one pence on a beer.

Yet we all have favourites. Going clockwise and in no particular order of merit, mine are the Costa Brava in Spain, Menorca, the Canal du Midi, Corsica and Sardinia, Sicily, the west coast of Italy from Naples down to the Strait of Messina, along the toe and heel of Italy, most parts of Greece and Turkey, and the bit of Morocco opposite Gibraltar.

2 Are there any uncrowded anchorages left?

Yes, but you need to look harder for them now, compared to 10 or 20 years ago. In the eastern Mediterranean there are areas that have relatively few boats even in the summer. Try cruising the eastern Sporades and northern Greece, some of the Cyclades, parts of the Gulf of Corinth and western Peloponnese, the Turkish coast from Kuşadasi north and the Sea of Marmara, the Turkish coast east of Antalya, southern Sicily and the west coast of Italy between Naples and the Strait of Messina, among the islands of Croatia (although it is crowded in high season), and parts of Tunisia. Many Continentals take their holidays en masse in July and August, so if you cruise early or late season in these countries it can feel positively deserted in places.

I'm always a bit surprised that some cruising folk arrange to sail in company along well known cruising highways and then complain that places are crowded. With a bit of planning, you can sail away from those yachting highways and will encounter far fewer yachts than in the more popular areas.

3 What about the winter?

Winters in the Mediterranean can be bitter and cold. It rains, hails, blows, snows and, in appearance, seems a very different place to the hot countries with azure water and blue skies that most of us visualise. Generally, people pack up around October and go home and venture out again in April. So if you are spending the winter on board make sure you have a good boat heater. If you have shore electricity supply, then a normal domestic fan heater works wonders.

It is possible to sail in the winter months, but you need to monitor the weather carefully and plan for ports of refuge for *when*, not *if*, it blows up. The eastern Mediterranean, and especially the Turkish coast, are better suited to winter sailing with lots of anchorages and harbours affording good protection and a fairly mild winter climate; although it still gets very cold and can even snow at sea level in exceptional years. For more information see Chapter 7, Weather.

4 What sort of boat is best?

The one you have, or the one that fits your budget and you can afford to maintain. There is no quick answer to this question, but Chapters 2 and 4 deal with some of the important features needed on a boat for Mediterranean cruising. In practice, lots of people – myself included – have sailed down to the Med in quite unsuitable boats but with luck and a little judgement, we have arrived safely and cruised extensively around the Mediterranean. Not that I recommend that you settle for an unsuitable boat, but if you really want to sail down there, then the important thing is the will to do so. I know of a Wayfarer dinghy, two Drascombe luggers, a kayak, and many 18–20-footers of varying vintages (among others) that have successfully cruised around the Med. And remember, the bigger the boat gets, the more it costs to run – that little equation can seriously influence budget considerations.

5 What sort of budget do I need?

Like the question above, there is no answer that is not a trite truism. In Chapter 5 I deal with some budget considerations that you are well advised to get a handle on. You will need some sort of income or savings, though not as much as you might think. I've always travelled on the basis of pulling my belt in another notch as money got tight, which meant that I could keep going on less and less. I will tell you that with adequate care it is a lot cheaper living on your boat in the Mediterranean than living in the UK. While you might have marina charges, hauling and boatyard charges, or the cost of a new sail or engine, what you do not have are all those expenses involved with running a car, a house, not to mention the cost of a mediocre bottle of wine; plus just try eating out in a restaurant once in a while. The UK is one of the most expensive countries in the world to live in whereas shopping or eating out in the Mediterranean is a fiscal joy.

6 Can I leave my boat down there?

Many people, including myself, are more or less permanently based in the Mediterranean. There are a lot more boatyards, yacht service companies and cheap flights these days; and a growing number of owners are choosing to base their boat in the Med instead of around the British coast. Given that the costs of berthing and hauling the boat are less than in the UK, while spares and repairs are around the same sort of price, throw in the cost of flights a few times a year, and the cost of keeping the boat in the Med adds up to about the same sort of figure as for the UK.

There are well-equipped boatyards scattered through most Mediterranean countries. This is the travel hoist at Cleopatra Marina in Preveza, Greece.

It is your choice whether you spend a few months at the beginning or end of the season or the whole season out there. But the attraction is that if you are in the Med in the settled summer season, you are more likely to be out on the water than sitting in the pub digesting a pork pie and the dire predictions of the weather forecast. Have a look at some of the options in Chapter 3 for more information.

7 Can I charter my boat?

Yes, but it can be an awful lot of trouble to do so. Around the Mediterranean, the regulations governing yacht charter vary from country to country. Within the EU there is no single ruling on charter regulations. Often you will need to get your boat surveyed and checked for safety equipment. You will also need to obtain certificates from the relevant government department to show that you are charter-legal, not to mention insurance – your normal insurance does not cover you for chartering. Then you will need some clients. Have a look at the section in Chapter 5.

There are a lot of big, well-organised and well-funded charter companies operating around the Mediterranean, and they have economies of scale that a one-boat operation cannot match. If you have a big yacht (minimum 50 foot) that is chic as opposed to homely, and someone who can produce haute cuisine while the boat is bashing to windward, then you could have a go at luxury yacht charter. Again, there is a lot of very good competition out there.

At times the wind will blow and you'll need to take the same sort of precautions as you would when cruising anywhere in the world. This is Ios in the Cyclades with the meltemi blowing into the bay.

One other alternative, which is looked at in Chapter 3, is to buy a yacht on a leaseback scheme. That means you don't have to bother with all the palaver of getting charter-legal and someone else looks after the yacht. You get to use it for a certain number of times in the year and at the end of the five-year lease you have a boat in the Mediterranean that is fully paid for.

8 Is the Mediterranean a safe place to sail?

Mostly yes. In all the EU countries, and some in between like Croatia and around to Turkey, you are less likely to be mugged or have something stolen off the boat than in the UK. Albania has seen some piracy incidents in the past, but with increased political stability the tourist industry is beginning to develop, and in turn yachts are slowly returning to Albanian waters. Italian and Greek naval vessels patrol here, looking for vessels carrying drugs or *clandestinis* (stowaways), and security in the towns and harbours is now good. In general, theft is on the increase but in many countries I still do not lock the boat up when going ashore. Most mugging and theft take place in a few hotspots like Malaga, Palma and Barcelona in Spain; or Corfu, Crete and Rhodes in Greece. A few places have acquired a reputation for theft from yachts and there has been something of an increase in rape figures in Greece and Turkey, though these mostly occur in some of the blighted tourist ghettos that have sprung up around the coast. On the North African coast, Egypt, Tunisia and Morocco are safe, but Algeria still has some unstable areas and is best avoided.

There have been some terrorist incidents aimed at tourists in Turkey, Israel, Egypt and Algeria, but in practice your chances of being a victim are probably less than in London.

9 Is there really too much or too little wind?

You often hear old Med hands sagely pronouncing that in the Med there is either too much or too little wind. At times it seems that it goes from flat calm to a force 7 in next to no time at all, but overall I think that this little homily has more to do with sloppy sailing skills and a reliable diesel. I see yachts motoring in perfectly good sailing breezes and it seems to me that the modern diesel engine has redefined sailing so that unless conditions are perfect and everyone on board feels like it, many yachts are choosing to motor when they could be sailing.

There is no doubt that the modern diesel has changed things. In *Roulette*, the 20-footer I sailed down to Greece, I had a 4 hp Stuart Turner that never started when you wanted it to and had enough fuel for a range of around 40 miles in a flat calm. In *Fiddlers Green*, a Cobra 850, I had a 12 hp Yanmar and enough fuel for a range of around 180 miles. In *Tetra* I had an 18 hp Volvo which was later replaced with an 18 hp Yanmar and a range of around 300 miles. In *seven tenths* I had a 32 hp Universal and a range of around 500 miles. In lots of ways this little history reflects the history of engines in sailing yachts over the last 25 years where the engine has gone from something that got you in and out of harbour and gave a bit of assistance in flat calms to something you turn on when you think your average speed has dropped below whatever predetermined speed you imagine the boat should be doing. The modern diesel has to some extent replaced sailing skills and I wonder just why some people go to the trouble of buying a sailing boat when what they really need is a motor boat.

10 What documentation do I need?

Requirements for documentation for the boat and the skipper have increased from 5 or 10 years ago. Documentation is dealt with in Chapter 5, but basically you will need the following:

Boat documents
- Part I or Part III registration.
- Proof of VAT payment (EU only).
- Ship radio licence.
- Boat insurance with a minimum of one million euros third party cover. Most countries require a translation of the third party cover.
- Some countries may ask for a current liferaft certificate and the ship's log.

Personal documents
- Valid passports.
- Visas can be obtained on entry for EU passport holders except for Syria, Libya and Algeria, although even here exceptions are made.
- Proof of competence to skipper a yacht such as the RYA Coastal Skipper or Yachtmaster qualification.
- You will need a radio operator's licence (Short Range Certificate for DSC VHF and Long Range Certificate for SSB radio).
- For European inland waterways you will need a CEVNI certificate (part of the International Certificate of Competence).
- Contact the RYA www.rya.org.uk for further information on boat and personal documentation.

2 | What Sort of Boat?

There is no such thing as the perfect cruising boat. The pros and cons of what comes close to the proper little ship could – and frequently do – fill a good sized book. What LOA? Long keel or fin? Spade rudder or skeg? Monohull or catamaran? Sloop or ketch? There are a lot of permutations to think about, but most of us are saved from dwelling too long on the matter by the simple constraints of our wallets, and the benevolence or otherwise of the bank manager. Or more usually, we already own a yacht that must perforce do the job.

If you already own a boat then you are pretty much there. Too often the dream sits locked in a file marked 'insufficient funds' with a brief to buy something 45ft long, all mod cons and enough space to swing a couple of cats. So often the file just sits there and the dream dims when in fact the boat you own or a more modest craft can do the job perfectly well. In these austere days a smaller boat has a lot of things going for it in terms of reduced berthing fees, less maintenance and less cost for replacement sails and the like. In many ways *Skylax* is too big for the job and we will down-size to something in the 38–42ft range in the future. And you get just as much joy out of a smaller boat as you do from the

MY CATALOGUE OF CRUISERS

The first yacht I sailed down to the Mediterranean, *Roulette*, was an early JOG (Junior Offshore Group) boat that looked all of 15 feet long although she was in fact 20 feet (6 metres). You could trail your hand in the water from the cockpit, and I only really realised how small she was when someone took a photo showing me standing in the cockpit. The coaming came about halfway up my shins. She was of hard-chine plywood construction, with moderate fin and a spade rudder and three-quarter rig. Auxiliary power was provided by a four horsepower Stuart Turner that once ran a water pump in 1944.

Roulette permitted sitting headroom only; she was narrow-gutted and hard-mouthed but she delivered me safely to Greece. The instrumentation was rudimentary to say the least: a grid-bearing main compass, a hand-bearing compass and a quickly acquired ability to judge the speed from the wake of the boat and the relationship between the colour of the water and depth.

My second boat was a modern 28-foot fin and skeg glassfibre sloop bought new from the factory, where I learned that a new boat can be as much of a problem as a second-hand one. *Fiddlers Green*

The first yacht that I sailed down to the Med, the 20-foot *Roulette*, seen here in Greece.

Tetranora was a traditional, long-keel boat built in the 1960s. She sailed like a witch but reversed with a mind of her own. (Photo Udo Hinnerkopf.)

was a teardrop shape when viewed from above; she had a high freeboard, wedge-shaped coachroof, numerous berths and boasted luxuries like a permanent chart table, shower, refrigerator, large galley and double berth. I sailed her down to Greece in a rather nasty winter and together we clocked up around 10,000 miles before I sold her in Athens.

In Athens I had fallen in love. *Tetranora*, sitting neglected in Kalamaki marina, was a 31-foot strip-planked boat designed and built in 1962 by Cheverton in the Isle of Wight. She weighed nearly twice as much as *Fiddlers Green*. By today's standards she had a narrow beam; she was long keeled, with a fine entry and a barn-door transom. Typical of her era, *Tetranora* had all the vices and virtues of the period, but together we clocked up tens of thousands of miles

including a trip to Southeast Asia and back.

seven tenths was a good all-rounder. A Cheoy Lee Pedrick 36 with moderate beam and weight, a long-fin keel and skeg-hung rudder, she had few vices and performed satisfactorily on passage. She did, however, have many virtues for warm-water cruising, including a good-sized cockpit, lots of opening hatches and ports and a big refrigerator.

My present boat *Skylax* is a Cardinal 46, which if anything is a tad too long. But then when you fall in love these things go by the board. She has a long fin keel with skeg and rudder, not too beamy compared with most modern boats and importantly is easily driven. Like *seven tenths* she has a good-sized cockpit, lots of ventilation and enough room for both of us to have separate working areas.

bigger model you kidded yourself would have that certain cachet and status in harbour.

The general guidelines that follow are no attempt to define that mythical beast, the perfect cruising yacht, but rather the yacht suited to Mediterranean cruising. A yacht designed to circumnavigate the world via the Southern Ocean is not necessarily the sort of yacht you want to have in the Mediterranean. For starters, you are hardly going to be sitting in the cockpit sipping sundowners in Tierra del Fuego, are you? So if you are considering purchasing a yacht for cruising around the Med, the following points should be borne in mind. On the other hand if you already own a yacht, do not be deterred from setting out as many – myself included – have done before in quite unsuitable but not unsafe craft.

When most people think of a cruising boat, an image of a heavy long-keeled boat similar to the Hiscocks' *Wanderer II* or to Moitessier's *Joshua* comes to mind. This is the legacy we are left with from the early years of cruising yachts and, while these will indeed make good cruising boats, they no longer come close to what a modern ideal cruising yacht is, or should be. There are a lot of heavy steel boats out there with bulletproof rigs and doghouses designed to withstand a 40-foot breaking wave, all designed and built to go around Cape Horn. The problem is that most of the owners aren't going around Cape Horn or any of the southern capes and many of these 'cape-horners' arrive in the Mediterranean with a boat that just doesn't suit the conditions there, or most low latitude cruising areas come to that.

Skylax is moderate to heavy displacement, with a slightly longer fin keel, when compared with modern cruising yachts

Displacement

Arguments about whether a cruising yacht should be heavy or light will be ongoing for decades. Over the last 20 years most production GRP boats have become lighter. Hull thickness has decreased and the weight of the interior furniture has been reduced through the use of moulded interiors for components like the galley and the heads, plus the use of plywood and veneers. Traditionally heavy items like the engine are now much lighter than marine engines of yore. Many of these production boats have been derived from racing yachts and, so the argument goes, they are unsuitable for extended cruising. They are not as safe as old-fashioned long-keeled boats in heavy weather and they are not as sea kindly.

For starters, most of these boats are as well-suited to Mediterranean and middle latitude cruising as those old-fashioned heavy cruisers. A lot of time is spent discussing what type of hull material and what thickness of hull is needed. If you look at some of the boats crossing oceans nowadays it would seem that most hulls can stand up to far more than we give them credit for. The most travelled couple I know have sailed just about everywhere including the north and south Pacific, Indian Ocean, Atlantic and the Mediterranean. They have sailed to some of these places not once but three or four times in a bog-standard Trapper 28 (old C&C 27). From my observations after years of cruising, most yachts have problems with gear and not with the integrity of the hull. Failures of rigging and engine, seacock and skin-fittings, boom (surprisingly common), rudders, torn sails, leaking windows and hatches, these are the sort of problems that most cruising yachts encounter and

ROUGH WEATHER

As far as I am concerned, a small yacht, whether heavy or light, is uncomfortable in rough weather. A heavy displacement long-keeled boat is no more comfortable in bad weather than a light displacement fin-keel yacht. The integrity of most modern yachts, whatever the weight, is rarely an issue and most of what goes on depends on how the crew handle any given situation. In the Mediterranean you will rarely be more than 20 miles from a safe harbour when cruising the coasts of the northern or southern Mediterranean. At times you could be 150 miles from the coast on longer crossings,

but this is the exception rather than the rule. Running before an ocean storm or heaving-to for 24 hours is the exception and you are only likely to get into this sort of pickle by sailing in the winter. This is not to say you will not encounter heavy weather in the Mediterranean – you will. The worst weather I have had after extended passages in the Indian Ocean or the Atlantic has been upon my return to the Mediterranean, though in every case I have been sailing out of season and in a hurry to get somewhere. And being in a hurry to get somewhere is just plain silly, wherever you sail.

not some intrinsic failure of the hull.

Above all else your boat must be easy to sail and perform well in light airs. This applies not only to the Mediterranean, but also to most other parts of the world. Whether you are in the Caribbean, Southeast Asia or in Australasia, you will have to cope with light weather unless you like turning your engine on all the time. A heavy boat that requires a force 5 to move it is depriving its owners of the best sailing – where you slip through the water at a couple of knots, under a gentle zephyr nudging you into a bay for the night. There are a lot of boats out there where the engine is turned on if the speed drops below 4 or 3 knots, or some other predetermined limit, and a lot of them are heavy displacement yachts of the 'cape-horner' type.

There is a common myth that lighter boats are quicker in light weather. In light winds a medium displacement boat will keep her way on without getting stopped easily, whereas light displacement boats are more easily stopped by the slightest bit of slop. A medium displacement boat with good light-weather sails can do very well in gentle winds. Crossing the Atlantic on the light-weather route, from the Leewards directly to the Azores, we used the asymmetric spinnaker on the moderate displacement *seven tenths* for nearly a week to bump speed up from around 2–3 knots to about 4 knots. A lot of yachts would have just turned the donk on and burned fuel.

What we are talking about in the end is design and, to some extent, the heavy or light argument does not come into it. There are a lot of heavy displacement boats around that are slow and difficult to sail for reasons of design. Likewise there are plenty of moderate to light displacement production boats that are slow and not especially easy to sail for no reason I can fathom, given that the design parameters for speed and easy tracking are well known to naval architects. There are heavy long-keel boats that are a joy to sail and perform well through a range of wind speeds. Likewise there are a lot of yachts of medium to light displacement that are fine sailing boats.

Size

Size is not everything. The overall size of your yacht is dependent on your financial position or, for some of us, on how far we can bend the bank manager's goodwill in extending an overdraft. That being so, I believe it is possible to buy a yacht that is too hefty for the average crew of two, usually a couple, to enjoy. While modern roller reefing on both the main and genoa means that quite large sails can be rolled or reefed using manual or electric and hydraulic systems, sailing the yacht is only part of it. In many cruising areas, like the Caribbean or the Pacific, you are mostly anchoring off and that is comparatively easy to do. You can motor up and let the electric anchor winch take the strain out of anchor handling. In the Mediterranean, however, you will often be berthing in quite small harbours or marinas, so boat handling in an enclosed space is something you will have to get used to. The bigger the yacht, the more stress there will be when berthing Med-style with the wind on the beam and someone on the dock bawling instructions at you.

In general, I believe that a medium displacement yacht nudging towards

seven tenths, a moderate displacement, long-fin keel cruising boat with plenty of opening hatches and ports for ventilation and good-sized cockpit for entertaining.

50 feet can become a liability. Even with modern sail management systems it will often be sailed without its best spread of canvas in case the wind gets up; the anchor and chain will be too hefty to get up by hand if the electric anchor winch breaks down; above and below decks, the gear is out of the realm of the makeshift repair category and, above all, berthing becomes a complicated affair. It is all very well when things are going right, but all too often they don't and with a yacht of this size, once the wind has taken charge when manoeuvring in a confined space, the consequences can be catastrophic.

It cannot be disputed that a yacht between 30 and 45 feet (9 to 14 metres) can be a seaworthy craft fit to voyage anywhere, as well as a comfortable and gracious home, but whether you can competently and comfortably handle a 50-footer (or bigger) without extra crew is open to question. Labour-saving devices may make it easy to hoist sail and haul anchor, but the sheer size of the craft has moved beyond the comfortable capabilities of a short-handed crew. If you rely on your family for crew, remember that sons and daughters may want to go their own way some of the time and eventually leave for good. Consequently, a family yacht should be well within the handling capabilities of a husband and wife.

Remember that sailing to, and around, the Med is not the same as sailing around the world with a few stopovers. In the Mediterranean you will spend a large part of your time in a harbour of some sort and that means you must be able to berth your yacht quietly and efficiently if it is not all going to turn into a nightmare. Many large yachts with small crews spend most of their time in one place because it becomes too much effort to take the boat out sailing for a day or two. The fun of sailing has been eclipsed by a floating home that can only occasionally go sailing.

A concluding thought: instead of buying the largest yacht you can afford, why not buy a slightly smaller, more manageable yacht and use the money saved for renting an apartment in whatever country you are in? In most Mediterranean countries during the off-season, accommodation can be cheaply obtained (with a bit of haggling) and you can leave the boat free for a refit. In this way you can have the best of both worlds.

Sailer or motor-sailer?

I've already mentioned the much received wisdom that in the Med it blows either too much or too little. I'll deal with this matter in a subsequent chapter, but the 'too much or too little' argument is often put forward to justify the choice of a motor-sailer as the best option for the Mediterranean. As far as I am concerned, it is another of those arguments that has been eclipsed by the availability of light and compact marine diesels.

RUNNING COSTS

	30ft	40ft	50ft
Basic Dacron mainsail (fully battened)	200ft²: £1300	400ft²: £2500	500ft²: £4200
Anchor (Delta)	10kg: £110	16kg: £170	25kg: £310
Calib. chain	40m/8mm: £220	60m/10mm: £500	80m/12mm: £1050
Inflatable dinghy and outboard	2.3m/2.5hp: £2000	3.1m/8hp: £3800	4.0m/20hp: £7000
1 night berth, Port Vell, Barcelona	€36	€50	€96
1 night berth, Kos Marina, Greece	€20	€28	€40
Haul and store for 6 months, Levkas Marina	€3200	€4900	€8500
Eroding antifouling (two coats)	20m²: £135/€150	40m²: £270/€300	62m²: £540/€500
12 months contract in Gouvia Marina, Greece	€3000	€4400	€6050

Note: Prices are not the best deals going and in many places are subject to haggling.

Diminutive 18-foot *Rozinante* is seen here in the Aegean after voyaging down the Danube and through the Black Sea.

A motor-sailer was once defined as a yacht that could motor faster to windward than it could sail. Most modern production yachts fitted with light, powerful diesels have this attribute and have consequently become, by definition, motor-sailers. The times have long gone when a 30- or 40-foot yacht was fitted with a spiteful 4 or 8 hp petrol engine that was used, when it could be coaxed into life, to get in and out of harbour. It is not uncommon now for a 35-foot yacht to have a 30+ hp motor, and many have considerably more powerful engines.

The term 'motor-sailer' is also generally accepted to mean that you have a sheltered 'driving' position, out of the wind, spray and rain. While being all in favour of sheltered steering, on every yacht there should be an outside steering

position as well. This is not just for visibility when manoeuvring under power (so you don't have to stick your head out of a hatch or door like a train-driver), but also because it can get very stuffy in an enclosed wheelhouse, no matter how many hatches you have. In harbour you will find that most motor-sailers and also those with the refined version of a pilot house will need to be fitted with canvas screens so that the glass doesn't act like a greenhouse and cause temperatures inside to soar. There is a certain irony here that having paid all that money for a pilot house, you have to cover it up in the summer and do without the view. A friend, who first sailed down to the Mediterranean in a motor-sailer, is selling it to get a boat with a good-sized outside cockpit. 'Like being in a glasshouse in the Sahara' is his verdict on enclosed deck cabins or pilot houses.

Whether your yacht is classified as a sailer or a motor-sailer, you will in any case need a reliable diesel with sufficient power to bash into the short choppy seas of the Mediterranean and to motor you economically through the calms. Looking back over the passage times for *Roulette*, my first yacht, which had a supremely unreliable 4 hp Stuart Turner, I find them to be agonisingly slow. Most passages over 100 miles were done at an average of 2 knots or so – enough said, unless you are exceptionally patient.

Design features

Most of the following features relate to all cruising boats, but some are specific to a Mediterranean cruising yacht and may

Skylax, my present boat, at 46 foot is if anything a tad on the large size, though at least the draught is kept to 2 metres so we can get into most places.

indeed be unsuitable in a world-girdler, or for cruising in more northerly waters.

Engines

You are going to be using the engine more than you would when sailing locally around your home waters. Some of the time you will be bashing into the Mediterranean chop to get into harbour and at other times you will be motoring in calms on passage. The engine will need to be in good condition and if it is not then you should think about installing a new one. There are far too many boats around that spend an inordinate amount

of time having expensive repairs done when the sensible thing would have been to install a new engine in the first place. I know, I have been there; spending money on an engine until it got to the point where I had spent as much as a new engine would have cost, except that I still had a tired, reconditioned engine.

If you are going to install a new engine, think about which ones have a good service network with easy access to spares. A less well-known marinised diesel may be cheaper to buy, but you may have to send home for spares. Getting hold of a service and spares manual is also worth the effort. In general there are good repair facilities across the Mediterranean and most spares are easily obtained.

Cockpits

A large cockpit is desirable because in the summer you will spend a good deal of your time there. It becomes, in effect, another room for reading, writing, eating, entertaining, sleeping or just plain relaxing. A roomy cockpit may not be ideal for the southern Ocean, but it is necessary in the Mediterranean for the alfresco life. A cockpit table is another essential piece of equipment but it should not be an elaborate affair that is a lot of trouble to put up. If you don't have a built-in cockpit table then a small wooden or pressed-steel table that folds flat is quite suitable, and it can often be stowed in a quarter berth or cockpit locker when not in use. Cockpit cushions are another good investment; they add greatly to your comfort, whether sailing or in harbour. They are best covered with vinyl or other PVC-backed material to stop water getting into the foam rubber, with a canvas or sturdy cloth over-cover for comfort and looks.

Cockpit stowage

Many modern yachts have a single cavernous cockpit locker so that you have to rearrange everything to get at the one thing you want in the bottom. Conversely, many centre cockpit yachts, which utilise the space under the cockpit and side-decks for living accommodation, have totally inadequate stowage. Remember that among other things you must find a home for diesel

cans, water cans, a length of hosepipe, gas bottles, engine oil, fishing tackle, not to mention fenders and warps. Good cockpit stowage is essential and you will need two or three cockpit lockers, which are not impracticably deep, for all the gear you will have to stow. Fender holders attached to the lifelines, pushpit or pulpit are also useful for keeping bulky fenders stowed and instantly ready for action.

Access

You will need good access not only to the engine, but to all the other bits of equipment that may need repairs when in constant use. This includes the generator, batteries, refrigeration unit, water pumps, toilet pump, holding tanks, bilge pumps and the fuel and water tanks. Too many modern yachts are built around equipment so that interior joinery or moulding must be removed to effect repairs.

Brightwork

Exterior varnish does not last well in the Mediterranean, where it will be constantly exposed to the sun and infrequently rinsed off by rain. The proportion of brightwork on a yacht quickly diminishes in direct proportion to the number of years spent in the Mediterranean. In my experience none of the new ultra-violet-resistant varnishes or oils can really cope with the sunny, salty conditions. My advice is to paint it!

Ventilation

You can't have too much. Most modern yachts are better ventilated than older yachts and it may be worth thinking

A roomy cockpit is an important feature because it is here you will spend most of your time and it needs to be big enough for entertaining as well.

about adding extra hatches and opening ports. *seven tenths* was 36 feet long and had two hatches in the forepeak, two hatches and four opening ports in the saloon, a hatch and an opening port in both the galley and the heads, and still the double quarterberth could have done with its own opening port.

Skylax has six hatches; two main hatches under spray hoods and twelve opening ports. Importantly the two main hatches can be left open except in the worst weather and the aft sleeping area has ventilation galore. If you have inadequate ventilation, then look at ways of cooling the interior in the section on ventilation in Chapter 4, Equipping the Boat.

Sail systems
Most yachts will come equipped with a roller furling headsail and an increasing number have an in-mast furling main. Personally I don't think you get a good set on the main with in-mast furling systems, even with vertical battens, and boat-for-boat, a well-cut main with slab reefing will leave an in-mast furling main for dead. In-boom furling systems are now a good deal more sophisticated than in days gone by, when you got a lumpy sail with a big bag in it, so this would be my choice if I was changing from a normal main. Whatever sail handling systems you have, make sure they have been checked over and that you have spares for any components that will wear. Most of the manufacturers can provide you with a spares kit if you request one.

Don't forget that your sails are going to get a lot more use and will be exposed to a lot more UV than in the UK. Roller reefing headsails should have a UV sacrificial strip and mains should have a good sail cover. For the main I have used an easy-stow sort of system (the manufacturers have a variety of names) whereby the mainsail cover is permanently on the boom and the main drops down between lazy-jacks into the cover. It can then be quickly zipped up or velcroed and protected from the sun before you have time to wonder whether or not to put on a normal sail cover.

Tankage
A lot of people worry about how much fuel and diesel to carry. Throughout most of the Mediterranean it is fairly easy to get water and fuel, so going to the expense of installing extra tanks is not really worth the effort. Water-makers need to be worked, and leaving it for the winter, even when all the preventative

maintenance and flushing and changing of filters is carried out as per the manufacturer's instructions, still won't guarantee you don't have problems when you come to start it up the next spring. If you are thinking of cruising off down the Red Sea or across the Atlantic after the Mediterranean then it may be worth thinking about installing a water-maker. These are a lot cheaper and more reliable than they used to be and even the 12 volt versions work remarkably well. I know of one 27-foot yacht that had a 12 volt water-maker installed and carried only a 100-litre water tank. Not something I do or recommend, but the yacht did complete a circumnavigation.

As far as diesel tanks go, unless your tank is spectacularly small it is usually not worth installing an additional tank. Very often diesel tanks are installed in the after sections of a yacht and add a lot of weight in the wrong place. Adding an additional tank there will only make matters worse. In the Mediterranean you will rarely be too far from somewhere you can fill up and as you may have to use jerry cans to get fuel in some places, it is worth carrying a couple anyway as an additional fuel supply.

Modifications and maintenance

After being in the Mediterranean for a season or two, you will probably decide to make some additions and modifications based on your newly acquired experience.

Commonly, it is reckoned that around 8–10 per cent of the value of the boat is a good figure for the running costs of the boat. Remember you will have insurance, marina and harbour charges, hauling and lay-up costs, running repairs and any replacement equipment. It always surprises me just how much it all adds up to and if something like an insurance premium shoots up (as it did in 2002, by a whopping 30 per cent), then it can severely dent a budget. Even if you do much of the work yourself, there are still all those inescapables like spare parts, antifouling, running rigging and that must-have new piece of electronic gimcrackery.

THE DESIRE TO GO

Human beings are endlessly ingenious at dreaming up reasons for choices that were never made. Far more important than acquiring the proper little ship for your voyage is the determination to go. We are all familiar with the stories of yachts equipped with every conceivable aid to navigation and safety being lost on a reef and of the impossibly small and fragile boats that successfully cross oceans.

Webb Chiles sailed his Drascombe Lugger *Chidiock Titchborne* across the Pacific and Indian Oceans before it was seized by the Saudis in the Red Sea. He took *Chidiock Titchborne II* to the Red Sea and then sailed on up and into the Mediterranean. I met him in Malta after he had sailed from Port Said to Valleta in 23 days and he seemed perfectly at home on this open 18-footer. I sailed *Roulette*, an old ply 20-footer, from the UK to Greece and many before and since have sailed similar sized yachts down there. Some really mad people have sailed things like a

Hobie Cat and a Wayfarer extensively in the eastern Mediterranean and I came across a German who sailed a kayak rigged with a sail and towed a small dinghy behind him with his equipment.

I don't really advocate that you should sail such craft, but the power of concentrated thought and an iron determination can accomplish much more than a sluggish spirit in the 'right' boat. One of my favourite tales of fantastic endeavour concerns a certain Fred Rebell. Forsaken in love, jobless in the great depression of the thirties, this extraordinary man decided to emigrate from Australia to America. Nobby Clarke tells the story in his book *An Evolution of Singlehanders:*

> 'The American Consul gave him little encouragement: waiting lists ... visas... immigration laws ... But Rebell had overcome such difficulties when he had left his homeland, and he was not deterred.
>
> He bought a clinker-built, three-quarter decked, 18ft centre-board sloop for £20, which was all the savings he had left. Finding a job building seaside cottages at the grossly underpaid rate of £1.50 per week, he managed to save some money – enough to buy some provisions for the projected voyage. He strengthened the boat by doubling the ribs and fixing an outside keel; he made a folding canvas hood to be fitted amidships for shelter;

he packed dried food into old paraffin cans fitted with screw caps, and took on board 30 gallons of water.

He taught himself to navigate by studying in the Sydney Public Library, and then, because navigation instruments were too expensive, he actually made a sextant and a distance-run log and purchased two cheap watches which he carefully rated. His charts were all traced from an elderly atlas in the library, so ancient that later he 'discovered' islands which had been unknown when the atlas was printed.

He left Sydney on December 31, 1931 and after a great many desperate adventures, including riding out a hurricane, he arrived at Los Angeles on January 7, 1933. The voyage of nearly 9000 miles in an open boat had taken exactly one year and one week. The total cost including boat, food and everything, came to £45. He did not even have to pay for a passport, since he issued his own: 'The bearer of this passport, Fred Rebell, of no allegiance, is travelling from Sydney, Australia via Pacific Ocean, United States of America and Atlantic Ocean to his native town, Windau, in the country of Latvia. Description of bearer: Sex: male. Age: 46 years. Height 5ft 8 in. Eyes: blue. Complexion: fair. Dated this 3 March, 1932.'

3 Mediterranean Cruising Options

Many people think of a cruise down to the Mediterranean as an 'all or nothing' voyage: you sail there, spend the winter on the boat, sail around some more and then return home. However, the reduction in air fares that has taken place in the last decade or more means that geographical distance is no longer the measure of where you can keep a boat and how you use it through the season.

All year round or part of the year?

Many people sell the house, car and granny and move their life on board a yacht. These are the live-aboards. Some of these people will cruise down to the Mediterranean as a full time option while some will see the Med merely as a stepping stone to cruising further afield. These are not the only options and many people now regard the Mediterranean as a place to keep a boat, a viable alternative to a marina close to home; so that, in effect, a marina in France or Greece can become your local marina. Instead of driving down a motorway to your marina, you now jump on a plane and fly to where your boat is kept. Plan it well in advance and the cost of the flight can be less than filling the car up with petrol.

Summer season

If you are retired, semi-retired or someone who can work through the winter to keep income rolling in, then using the boat for the summer is a perfectly viable option. Many owners choose to sail in the summer and haul the boat out in a yard for the winter; this is what I generally do. The Mediterranean can be surprisingly cold in the winter, especially if northerlies blow down off the Arctic; and while it is possible to sail at this time, it is not as warm as you might think.

I am often asked where I am going to leave my boat for the winter and the truth is I don't always know. There are enough boatyards scattered around the Mediterranean for you to have a good choice when you arrive somewhere and it is rare not to be able to find a place. Sometimes you may have to detour 30 or 40 miles along the coast to find a yard that has space and suits your pocket, but usually you will have been taking notes from other cruising people en route and will have a couple of boatyards picked out for inspection.

Getting back home from wherever you leave the boat can sometimes be a problem, although because of low air fares you can usually get there and back for very little. Normally you will have a fair idea of when you want to travel out to the boat and when you will be coming back, so it is possible to book well in advance. The low cost airlines offer cheap seats for booking in the first tranche of 10 or 20 seats on the plane, after which there is an incremental rise for successive tranches of seats (see page 30). They offer such good value that is often worth booking in advance even if you are not sure you will use it. Ryanair, easyJet and Flybe offer these sorts of deals and make access to the boat very affordable.

Alternatively, many charter airlines operate in the summer to popular holiday destinations and a return flight (even though you don't use the return half) can work out a lot cheaper than regular scheduled flights. Look around the internet for cheap flights, or browse your Sunday paper and phone around. It's surprising what sort of deals you can get. When returning home, you can often find good deals through local travel agents. They may be able to buy you a return flight on a charter airline or negotiate cheap, late deals on regular scheduled flights. If you leave your boat in a country such as Tunisia or Morocco where it is less easy to find cheap flights, you can get a ferry across to say Malta or Gibraltar and fly home on a cheap flight from there.

Part-time summer options

An increasing number of people are basing a yacht in the Mediterranean and going out for relatively short periods several times throughout the year. The most popular options are to use the boat for a month or two in the spring and again in the autumn which avoids the hot, busy summer period. During the summer, the boat can be left in the water on a mooring, in a marina, or you can haul it out. A number of boatyards offer good deals on multiple (usually 4 or 6) hauling and launching in the same year. After the autumn cruise, the boat can be hauled for the winter.

If you choose this option it would be advisable to employ an individual or company that provides *gardiennage* services. There is no reason why you cannot leave the boat unattended in a secure marina until your return, but you will need to schedule in some extra time to get things in working order and to arrange for any urgent repairs. The advantage of having someone looking after your boat is that over the winter, any repair jobs or cosmetic details can be attended to and in the spring the boat can be commissioned and antifouled ready for launching. Many of these companies will have your boat launched and ready to go when you arrive. So you can literally step aboard and start your spring cruise. Alternatively you can spend a week or two commissioning the boat yourself and getting it launched and berthed somewhere.

Finding a reliable individual or company to look after your boat can be a difficult job. There are any number of cowboys out there willing and able to siphon money from you in return for very little. This is another instance of when spending time asking others about their experiences with *gardiennage* will pay dividends. Eventually you will end up with a good shortlist of recommendations. Ideally, you should deal with an individual or company with an established reputation, and not just choose someone friendly who has decided

There are marinas both large and small all around the Mediterranean, so you can base your yacht there and fly out whenever you fancy cruising for a month or so. This is Levkas Marina, about 30 minutes from Preveza Airport.

that looking after boats for the winter will be a good little earner. There is no guaranteed success for any of this, but with a little informal research and a bit of careful judgement you will ferret out the good from the bad.

Some owners opt to keep their boat in a marina through the winter and then get it hauled for a week or so in the spring to clean off the bottom and antifoul it. I think it is a better option to haul every winter so that the boat is safely out of the marine environment and away from possible damage afloat. More importantly, a GRP boat hauled for the winter has time for the hull to

dry out. All GRP boats absorb some water through the gelcoat. Even if your boat has epoxy paint over the top of the gelcoat, it will still absorb some water for the simple reason that neither gelcoat nor epoxy paint are 100 per cent waterproof. Boats that are regularly hauled for the winter have much less chance of developing blisters and damaging the glass mat core. Yachts that sit in the water year in and year out commonly suffer from osmosis problems, no matter how carefully the hull has been built. The first charter boats I ran in the Mediterranean, some 33 years ago, were not the most brilliantly constructed boats

Keep your boat in the South of France and you can fly to Marignane airport near Marseille and cruise areas like the nearby Calanques. This is Calanque d'en Vau between Marseille and Cassis.

and were not built using isophalic resins. Those boats have been hauled every winter and, to my knowledge, none have developed osmotic blisters. My last boat *seven tenths* sat in a marina for five years or so through summer and winter; when I first acquired her, she had a higher moisture content in the hull than I would have liked, though not so bad it needed attention. After being hauled for a number of winters, the moisture content reduced significantly. Likewise, my current boat *Skylax* had been sitting neglected in a marina for years and the moisture content in the hull is now much less after just a few winters on the hard.

Some owners with a boat based in the Med will sometimes pop out for as little as a week or two. The availability of those cheap flights means that this is perfectly feasible. As air travel gets even cheaper, which it surely will, due to an even greater proliferation of low-cost-no-frills airlines flying to Mediterranean destinations, then the possibility of keeping a boat in the Med as an option to keeping it in home waters will become even more realistic.

TIPS FOR LOW COST FLIGHTS

Getting a low cost flight really boils down to research – and a bit more research. Don't accept that X pounds is what you will have to pay until you are quite sure that it is the bottom line.

- Use the internet. All the low cost airlines like easyJet, Ryanair and others have websites where you can check out prices for future dates. There are also numerous cheap flight sites where discounted prices on scheduled flights with national airlines and charter flights can be found. Often there are deals on the internet you will not find elsewhere.

- Look through the travel sections of the Sunday papers. Ring around and mention you have got a price of X pounds from one company: can they do better?

- Try to be flexible with your departure or return dates. With low cost airlines you might find that a flight on a Tuesday is much cheaper than a Monday flight when people are returning from a weekend away. On charter flights you might find one flight is full while another is not and that the operator is prepared to do deals on the empty flight.

- With low cost airlines, book early. Six months or more is not too early although it does fix your journey time to a certain date. Low cost airlines work by selling off the first 10 per cent of seats at say £25, the next 10 per cent at £45, and so on up to the last 10 per cent at say £200, although the progression is usually not linear and you might find the price differentials and percentage of seats vary in the middle price range. If you change the date of a low cost seat then you will have to pay the current price difference at the time you alter it, and a booking fee.

- Charter flights will always be full during school holidays and the peak summer season. Depending on how bold and how flexible your plans are, leave booking the flight until as close to departure time as possible. Prices are discounted closer to the flight time as an operator tries to get some money back on the block of seats he has contracted to buy.

- You don't always have to fly direct to where your boat is located. Most countries have relatively inexpensive internal flights so if you can fly to a main airport and then take an internal flight to where your boat is, it can save you a lot of money. For example, you can fly to Athens with easyJet and then take an internal flight from Athens to Preveza in the Ionian rather than flying direct to Preveza.

- For France, northern Italy and Spain, remember that there are fast rail links. Alternatively you can drive down.

Buying a boat in the Med

It is possible to buy a new or second-hand yacht from marinas or boatyards around most of the northern Mediterranean. This way you can have your yacht exactly where you want it without the hassle of sailing it there – increasingly this is becoming a popular option.

Buying new

There are a number of dealers for yacht builders, such as Beneteau, Jeanneau, Dufour, Hanse, Elan and Bavaria, scattered around the northern Mediterranean from Spain through to Greece and Turkey. You can find the retailer details either from the builders themselves or from the internet and then contact the dealer direct regarding the yacht you are interested in. Because you are buying from a main dealer there should be no problems with security of funds or with the commissioning of the yacht and paperwork for the country you are in. You may find it difficult to resolve issues over equipment, commissioning, costs etc at a distance as it will probably not be possible for you to pop out frequently to check on progress. It is essential you leave a week or more free during the handover of the boat so that any problems can be resolved there and then.

If you are not buying from an authorised main dealer then you need to be very careful over selecting a broker. Check how long the company has been in business, whether they belong to a professional body and, if possible, get personal recommendations.

An alternative to buying a new boat from a dealer in the Mediterranean is to buy it new in the UK and have it delivered to a location in the Med. This way you negotiate with the dealer in your own country where it is easier to safeguard your money and to check on credentials; also the dealer can arrange delivery. You should ensure that the yacht is delivered to a suitable marina where it can be adequately commissioned and any shortcomings speedily repaired.

Buying second-hand or 'pre-owned'

There are brokers in most countries around the northern Mediterranean and you will find a good choice of yachts offered for private sale in harbours and yards scattered all around the Med. Most of the brokers are reputable, having well established businesses, but you will need to check how long they have been in business and whether they are known to the trade or can supply testimonials that you can check. You can track down brokers on the internet, and many advertise in yachting magazines.

A number of charter companies in the Mediterranean, such as Sunsail and the Moorings, sell their charter yachts after five years or so. These yachts will almost invariably have been supplied by some of the big boatbuilders and will be to charter specifications, which often means that they come with all sorts of extras. Although, as charter boats, they will have had a hard life, with an adequate maintenance schedule they can be good buys. Often it will have a better maintenance schedule than a private yacht, which may have been sitting around for a while before the owner decided to sell. Usually some items like sails and canvas will have to be replaced, but this is usually taken into account in the asking price.

If you are buying from a private seller then things are not so straightforward. If possible, do the deal in the UK and get everything properly documented. It is normal for an inventory to be supplied so you should check that everything listed is present on the boat and any promises, such as the life raft to be serviced or the

Some charter companies sell their yachts on after four or five years so you can pick up a used yacht, fully equipped for Mediterranean cruising (probably fairly well maintained), which is already out there – ready for you to sail away.

yacht launched, are carried out before your final payment. Once you have paid the balance of a purchase price it can be surprisingly difficult to track down the vendor to get any outstanding problems rectified.

Document checklist

The following points should be remembered when purchasing a new or used yacht in the Mediterranean.

- VAT on all EU registered yachts has to be paid in all EU countries. If no proof of VAT payment is obtained, then you will be liable for VAT in the country of purchase, except if you are exporting it to a non-EU country. A yacht purchased outside the EU, regardless of whether VAT has previously been paid, will be liable for VAT when re-imported to the EU.

- EU yachts on which VAT has been paid and which have spent 3 years or more in non-EU waters have incurred problems with their VAT status when returning to the EU. UK guidelines suggest that, provided the yacht is under the same ownership and not permanently exported, but on a voyage, it is therefore not being re-imported, and VAT paid status is retained. These guidelines may be interpreted differently in other EU countries, and should not be assumed.

- All yachts imported into the EU since June 1998 must comply with EU RCD (Recreational Craft Directive) regulations. Recently built yachts will usually be RCD compliant and have a CE mark. Yachts built outside the EU, before the RCD regulations were introduced, can be assessed retrospectively although this is expensive. (More information about the RCD can be obtained from the Technical Unit of the RYA.)

- Apart from the ownership and/or registration papers for the yacht, you will need the requisite documentation including things like passports, insurance papers, a certificate of competence and in some cases a radio licence. A second-hand yacht may need to be taken off the registry of one country and either Part 1 or Part 3 registration for UK yachts obtained. It is worthwhile getting the broker to remove it from the registry for you as, for some countries, this can be a tedious and long-winded business.

- A new boat should not need a survey, but get a surveyor to run his eye over the boat to make sure everything is in order. To some extent, you will be protected by the manufacturer's warranty although the methods of rectifying problems may be better determined by a surveyor. If you are purchasing a second-hand yacht, then I strongly recommend that you have it fully surveyed. Any yacht over 10 years old will usually need a survey to satisfy your insurer. There are Lloyds approved surveyors in most countries,

or you can contact the YBDSA (Yacht Brokers, Designers and Surveyors Association), the professional body for approved members in a particular country. Some British surveyors do regular runs to various parts of the Mediterranean and you can be included on a 'tour', which will cut costs somewhat, or you can pay for airfares and hotels, plus the survey fee, for an individual visit.

- The broker should supply a Memorandum of Agreement detailing what is to be paid when and how and also any conditions such as 'subject to survey'. If possible your money should be held in an escrow account.

DELIVERY TO THE MEDITERRANEAN

At one time I made a living delivering boats to and around the Mediterranean. It is not an easy job and yacht delivery companies earn every penny they charge. Most companies choose to deliver yachts via Biscay and in through the Strait of Gibraltar, although a few will deliver smaller boats down through the French canals. There are a lot of reliable companies that can be tracked down in the classified ads of the yachting magazines or over the internet. However, you should get a word-of-mouth recommendation, as yachts can take quite a beating from a sloppy delivery crew. A good company will inspect the boat, leaf through the maintenance schedule and check the spares and equipment on board. They will then arrange a delivery schedule with you, which will obviously depend on the prevailing weather conditions and will have a plus or minus factor built into it.

For a 12-metre yacht, in good condition and equipped for the voyage, the current fee for a delivery from a southern UK port to the Balearics would be around £3000. This cost is based on a skipper, first mate and one crew, a number of days' preparation and the actual delivery trip. Any additional days – through bad weather or necessary preparation on the yacht – would cost around £125 per day.

Some delivery companies are happy to have the owner on board (OOB) for the delivery, although others will not. If you feel you do not have the experience to do the trip down to the Mediterranean on your yacht, then having a skipper and crew on board will help your skills and boost your confidence for future trips.

A number of companies will transport yachts overland to most destinations around the northern Med. When I was running a charter company, we had the boats trucked two at a time from the UK to Brindisi on the heel of Italy, and then sailed them across to Greece. It proved to be a quick and efficient way of getting the yachts to the charter base. Expect to pay around £4500–£6000 for a 40-foot yacht plus any craning, ferry and motorway tolls. Many companies specialise in overland deliveries, and a number of boatyards on the French and Italian coast will arrange this, including re-stepping the mast and launching. Over 45 feet it is more cost efficient to deliver the yacht on its own bottom via Biscay.

There are also a number of companies that deliver yachts on board a ship. To deliver a 40-foot yacht from the south of England to Palma, Mallorca as deck cargo would cost in the region of £4500–£5000.

You can cut costs by being flexible about times and destinations. For example, you may be able to arrange for delivery by land on a back-to-back basis when a truck has an empty slot. Likewise you may be able to do a back-to-back delivery leg so that a delivery crew does not need to fly home.

Of course it is possible to deliver the yacht to the Med yourself. The three main routes are through the French canals from Northern France (draft restrictions will apply in some canals); around Ushant and then through the French canals from Bordeaux (max recommended draft 1.6m) or taking the sea route across Biscay and into the Med via Gibraltar – either as a leisurely cruise or a quicker offshore passage.

Boat-sharing

Forming a syndicate of like-minded individuals to buy and run a boat makes a lot of sense for anyone who wants a boat part-time in the Med. The initial cost of the boat and the running costs are reduced to half, a quarter or a sixth, depending on the number of people in the scheme. Boat-sharing is nothing new, but for a successful partnership there are some simple rules to be followed.

The partners
They are the key to the whole business and can make or break a boat-sharing syndicate. If the partners disagree about what is happening to the boat, bicker over where it should be based for the season, and are dissatisfied with the way the other partners treat the boat, the scheme isn't going to work. Boat-sharing has to be an amiable arrangement with a fair amount of tolerance built into it, rather than just a business arrangement to get a percentage of time afloat.

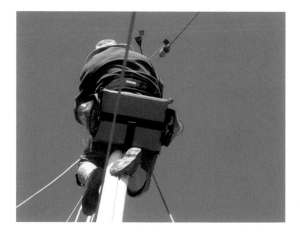

With a boat-sharing syndicate it is important that work on the boat is carried out equally and all members pull their weight.

The number of people in the partnership should depend on how much time you all intend to spend on the boat. The ideal arrangement would be 2, but 4 is probably the most practical with 6 around the maximum that you want. Syndicates do exist with 10 or 12 partners, but the grumbling from syndicates of this size is always audible and the boat suffers from group neglect because no one feels any real responsibility for it. All the partners should get on well and be able to afford not only the initial cost, but the running and ancillary costs as well. They should have similar sailing experience and common aims for the use of the boat. It is no use putting together someone who wants a state-of-the-art racing machine with a retired couple who want a sedate shallow-draught cruising boat to potter around creeks and bays. Nor should the partners all have school-age children, or everyone will want to use the boat during the school holiday periods. Indeed you need some partners who positively prefer to cruise in the early or late season.

It is a tall order to get four or six totally like-minded people together for this sort of scheme, and this is where the tolerance bit comes in. The partners in the scheme must be prepared to absorb the foibles of others without letting anything rub them up the wrong way. Most partnerships have dissolved, not because boat-sharing was impractical, but because Joe didn't replace the broken crockery or Fred didn't clean the shower tray properly. Partners in a boat-sharing syndicate must understand that they have a share in a common boat and therefore a share in the idiosyncrasies of the other

syndicate members. Some syndicates have written rules and instructions on the operation of the yacht and its equipment, but I'm not sure whether rules and regulations are necessary if you have the right mix of partners and good communication between them. It may be that too rigid an organisation will prevent full utilisation of the boat, and worse, take the fun out of it.

Setting up

One thing that is of the utmost importance is that no boat-sharing syndicate should be set up, even between life-long friends, without a formal, written, legal document that all the partners will sign. The RYA publish a suggested form of agreement which provides a guide to the sort of agreement to be drawn up. The final document should detail the shares of the partners, what expenditure requires prior approval by the syndicate, and what the wider responsibilities of the partners are.

While the document should spell out the whys and wherefores of the syndicate, it should not be overly constricting on matters such as where the boat is to be based or how the boat is to be maintained. It may be that the syndicate decide to move the boat for a year or two to another country in the Mediterranean, or even that it is necessary to do so to avoid import or luxury taxes specific to a country (in Mallorca, for example, you may be charged a 12 per cent wealth tax after 183 days there). Maintenance is something that can vary annually, so that one year the minimum maintenance is necessary, while in the next it gets a good refit.

The choice of boat for the syndicate will vary depending on the desires and needs of the partners. Most boats in boat-sharing syndicates are middle-of-the-road cruisers between 10 and 12 metres, but there is no reason why a syndicate should not buy a racing yacht or a 20-knot planing power boat. The boat should be of glassfibre construction for easy maintenance, and all the gear must be reliable and sturdy. The engine will cause more problems than any other part of the boat, and a major breakdown will not only cost the syndicate money, but can jeopardise the holidays of other members.

The boat should be under the flag of the country in which the partners live, with all the names on the registration and ownership papers. If any of the names of partners are omitted from the ownership papers, the syndicate will run into trouble in most of the countries in the Mediterranean, as the authorities will then assume that the boat is being chartered. It is no use pleading ignorance and proffering bits of paper that show you are a syndicate member – they want to see your name on the ownership and registration papers and if it is not there, the boat will be held up, fined, or may even be impounded.

Setting up a boat-sharing syndicate is not as easy as putting an advertisement in a magazine for partners, buying a boat, and sailing it down to the Mediterranean. The scheme needs planning and careful consideration over the choice of partners. Having pointed out the pitfalls, I should add that boat-sharing makes real sense, offering not only economy, but introducing you to a group of people

that are likely to become good friends. One syndicate I know holds an annual ball for partners and friends. Don't be put off if one syndicate doesn't work out for you, as you can start again, learning from the mistakes of the previous one.

Timeshare

A number of years ago, timeshare advertisements were splashed all over the national newspapers and glossy magazines: 'Sail your own boat in Spain, or France, or Greece, for two weeks of the year, every year, for a once only payment of 'X' number of pounds. Get a villa to go with it for two weeks of the year, for only another 'X' number of pounds.' There are fewer advertisements now, but timeshare companies are still around although often under different titles – timeshare has become syndicated yacht ownership, share yacht ownership, syndicated boatshare, or whatever mix of words can be dreamed up.

Basically, timeshare is what it says it is: you buy a share in a boat for an amount of time, commonly two weeks, for a lump payment. You can then use the boat every year for that period until the boat is sold and the proceeds are shared out to the timeshare customers. Prices for your share vary according to the time of year you opt for, with high season the most expensive scaling down to the least expensive periods at the very beginning and end of the season. The timeshare company owns and maintains the boat and can sometimes arrange cheap flights.

It sounds like a good idea, but in practice there are a lot of problems. There

Choosing the right base for the boat needs careful consideration. This is Portomaso Marina in Malta – an excellent base for easy access to the east or west Mediterranean.

were many cases of companies going bankrupt a short time after selling most of the options, often in suspicious circumstances. After the receiver had paid off all the companies' primary debtors, there was little left for the timeshare customers – no boat, no money, and no holiday for the next 10 or 15 years.

A number of the companies still in business have not maintained the boats in good condition and you don't have to look far to find dissatisfied customers who became unhappy with the condition of the boat after a year or two. One of the problems was that the small print gave the company the freedom to charter the boat to cover any slots that were not filled

by timeshare customers, and so the boat got bashed around on charter as well as being poorly maintained.

Recently an auction of unwanted timeshares took place that demonstrated how unsatisfactory some options have been. Of the timeshares up for auction, only 20 per cent sold and all of these fetched less than 50 per cent of the original price. Many of the owners of the timeshares were selling them because they could not use the option in the allotted period, nor could they exchange the period for other dates as they had been led to believe. Also, with maintenance charges due every year as well as repayments on the timeshare itself, the financial burden had become too great for a very small return in the pleasure they thought they were buying. The Department of Trade and Industry has been looking into timeshares and the companies selling them (often with high-pressure sale techniques), with the aim of establishing a code of practice and legal guidelines. At present their advice is not to sign anything until you are sure of what you are doing and what the whole financial commitment is, and always ensure that you have a 'cooling off' period after the initial commitment where you can change your mind and opt out of the agreement.

There are few competently managed timeshare companies still in business and selling options on boats. If you are contemplating buying an option, go out and look at the boats. Do not put up with being shown a boat 'like' the one you will get – demand to see the actual boat you will share. And if it fails, you can join the large number of other people who trade timeshares with one another; a trade so big that several companies have been set up to deal with reject timeshares. One timeshare owner of a boat summed up his feelings on timeshare companies like this: 'Avoid them like the plague – unless you happen to own the management company'.

Leaseback

A number of charter companies operate leaseback schemes whereby you buy the boat and the charter company leases it back from you. Most leaseback schemes operate over a five year period, after which the company sells the boat or you can take it over. It works something like this:

- You buy the boat, say a charter-equipped Bavaria 36, at something like £90,000 (2011). You will have to put around £30,000 down and pay the £60,000 balance at, typically, 8–10 per cent which over 5 years will be £16,000 per annum.
- Typical income over a 5-year period from 15–18 weeks in the season would be around £30–£40,000 although there are a lot of variables at work.
- At the end of the 5-year period you will fully own the boat which will usually have a residual value calculated at around 60 per cent of its new cost (£54,000 on the Bavaria 36).
- Included in the deal will be use of the boat by the owner, usually for two weeks in the high season and up to four weeks in the low season.
- The leaseback company is responsible for all maintenance, insurance, registration and harbour fees.

Leaseback schemes are best viewed as a way of keeping a boat in the Med without all the hassle and expense of getting it there and maintaining it. The charter company will look after it and all you do is arrive on the dock and step aboard. At the end of the two weeks you simply hand it back. After five years you will own the boat or the company can sell it and you will get some capital back. After keying in the worth of the owner's use of the boat over five years, net returns are probably around 10 per cent.

There are a number of things to bear in mind with leaseback deals to avoid pitfalls as with the timeshare option:

- You must choose a reputable company. Large companies like Sunsail, Moorings and Kiriakoulis all operate these schemes and so do a number of smaller companies. If possible, have a chat with someone who has been involved in a leaseback scheme.
- Make sure your name is on the registration documents as 100 per cent owner.
- If the charter company operating the leaseback goes bankrupt, theoretically you can step in and reclaim your boat. In practice this may not be that easy as unpaid local creditors will want a share in your boat to cover their bills.
- A charter boat will get about four to five times the amount of use a private boat is put to, much like a hire car, so there will be a lot of wear and tear.

That said, charter companies have to keep their boats working well and looking good, so regular maintenance is usually carried out.

Try it out

Not everyone likes the reality as much as the dream. Before you spend a large amount of money buying a boat, or getting involved in something like a boat-share or leaseback scheme, it is a good idea to take everyone involved on a charter holiday in the Mediterranean to see if they like it. Some charter companies have delivery cruises at the beginning and end of the season and this is an opportunity to do a lot more miles to or from the winter base to the charter area. Also, spending two or three weeks living very closely together onboard in a foreign country will be a new experience for many families and couples – sometimes it does not pan out.

Some boat owners put the boat in the water in the spring and haul it for July and August before going back out again and putting it back in the water in the autumn. This can work out less expensive than leaving it in a marina berth.

4 Equipping the Boat

This chapter does not pretend to cover all the equipment you will need on a boat. That would be a book in itself. What I'm looking at here is equipment pertinent to cruising in the Mediterranean. Some of the topics like biminis or ventilation might be considered a bit trite to get such prominence, but trust me, these are probably much more important items for warm-water cruising than a colour radar or chart plotter.

Anyone who owns a boat knows that it is never completely ready. There is always more equipment you can add, and there is always maintenance to be done. There are a small number of yachts that put to sea in a totally unseaworthy condition with owners who seem to have little or no conception of what sailing and navigating are about; conversely, there is also that much larger group of owners who believe that a yacht must be so elaborately equipped that they spend the best years of their life preparing it, instead of being out on the water enjoying it. Most of us sail on, knowing that we *really should* service the sticky morse controls or replace that saggy mainsail; and it will be a miracle if that cooker lasts another season. In the Mediterranean you will be able to find spares and repair facilities for most items on board and at around the same cost as (and sometimes cheaper than)

the UK. So don't think you need to have everything perfectly installed and ready to go before you leave home, as you can replace and add bits just as easily in the Mediterranean.

Cruising has often been described as 'fixing the boat in exotic locations' and there is a lot of truth in that. I'm not advocating you set off in an unsafe boat without the equipment and knowledge needed to get you safely to the next harbour or anchorage. What I am saying is that you should remember that there is no final coat of varnish; no hull that doesn't show the wear and tear of visiting new harbours; no sail that doesn't need repairs or engine that does not need an overhaul; no electronic equipment that is the final state of the art; no navigation

Cruising: 'Fixing the boat in paradise' they say.

lesson that removes the uncertainty of a landfall, and nothing that will contain one's fear at the height of a gale – although a hot drink helps.

With this caution in mind, look over this chapter with a sceptical eye and decide what it is reasonable and affordable to do. The rest you can catch up with along the way.

Biminis and awnings

It astounds me that there are still boats sailing around the Mediterranean without a permanent bimini shading the cockpit. In the Caribbean you rarely see a boat without a bimini that is left up most of the time. One of the questions I am frequently asked is whether I leave mine up all the time. Yes I leave it up all the time, unless the wind gets up to 45 knots plus. On the entire passage to Southeast Asia and back in *Tetra*, the bimini was up all the time. For the Caribbean and the Atlantic crossing on *seven tenths*, the bimini was only taken off once, when Hurricane George threatened Fort Lauderdale. For some reason, even in quite strong gusts, biminis seem to remain stable, as the wind mostly pushes down on it rather than trying to blow it up and off.

Most canvas makers will make up the stainless steel work for a folding bimini, or will know someone who can. Large chandlers can usually supply or order the fittings for the bimini metalwork so you can buy stainless steel tube fabricated to size and then simply bolt it all on yourself. Alternatively, you can design and make your own out of cheaper materials. For years I cruised in *Tetra*

If the central panel of the spray hood is fitted with zips, you can open it up to allow the breeze to cool the cockpit.

with a permanent galvanised pipe affair that did not fold down but cost virtually nothing to construct.

One addition to the standard bimini that is worth considering is add-on side curtains for when the sun is low in the sky. On *Tetra* I had curtains that rolled up and were secured in place with velcro. When you wanted a bit more shade you rolled a curtain down and tied it off to the lifelines. With a bit of judicious planning, a large solar panel can provide shade for the helmsman when mounted behind a bimini. More up-market biminis have a zip or poppers to attach side or back screens.

Apart from the bimini, you will need a larger awning to put up in harbour or at anchor. This can extend over the bimini as the double layer will cool the cockpit even more and keep below decks cool as well. I favour awnings that have a pole through either end so the awning can be simply tied on with a few bits of string rather than 'tent' type awnings

Slip on a shirt, slop on sunblock and slap on a hat.

which must be secured in several places to the lifelines. In addition, the 'tent' type awning restricts access along the side-decks whereas using an awning supported by poles means that you don't have to bend double to get along the side-decks. Plumbers' grey plastic piping makes good poles to go through a hemmed awning as you can bend them a little when tying the awning down; this makes it less prone to wind getting under it. Like biminis, you can have side curtains which attach to the awning when the sun is low in the sky.

One other thing that helps to keep the cockpit cool is to have the central clear panel of a sprayhood made with zips so that you can roll it up to get some through breeze. This also helps to increase visibility when coming into harbour if, for some reason, you want

Canvas everywhere and lots of opening hatches and ports makes for a cool boat in the hot Mediterranean summer.

PROTECTION FROM UV RADIATION

Skin cancer has increased dramatically in recent years, mostly because of the fashion for sunbathing on holiday and returning home with a tan. On a yacht you are at an increased risk of skin cancer because ultraviolet radiation is reflected off the water. Ultraviolet rays in sunlight increase the production of a protective pigment called melanin which gives the skin its brown colour. However, even with the temporary increase of melanin, the tan does not prevent penetration of the skin by UV rays which can be extremely damaging.

There are three types of UV radiation: UVC, UVB and UVA, but it is mostly UVA that we have to worry about. UVA is largely unaffected by the ozone layer and penetrates deeper into the skin than UVB.

The main risk factors for skin cancer are over-exposure to UVA and skin colour. Individuals with fair or freckled skin burn easily. Dark skins are at lower risk although they are still in danger from skin cancer.

There are a number of things you can do to decrease the risk of skin cancer. The Australian slogan 'Slip, Slop, Slap' encapsulates the best advice:

- **Slip** on a shirt. It is important to know that a lot of fabrics like white cotton do not stop all the UVA hitting you. Darker fabrics and some specially designed shirts will cut out a higher percentage of UVA.
- **Slop** on sunblock or suntan cream. Depending on your skin colour this should be a high factor SPF cream (at least factor 30 and preferably higher). For areas commonly exposed, like the face and hands, use total sunblock.
- **Slap** on a hat. Wearing a good sun hat with a wide brim should become second nature. There are plenty of hats around with a good brim and a strap to hold it on when there is some wind. Baseball-type caps give some protection but not as much as a proper brimmed hat. Sailing gloves are also useful to protect the back of your hands from skin damage. I only wish I had worn them in earlier sailing years even if it doesn't feel like you are a proper roughtie-toughtie sailor with them on.

In addition to this advice, think about the following:

- On a boat, a bimini protects you from a lot of UVA although some is still reflected off the water. A permanent bimini will radically decrease exposure to UVA in the cockpit.
- In harbour or at anchor, an awning cuts down on UVA exposure.
- If you are snorkelling, wear a T-shirt and waterproof sunblock, or your back and the backs of your legs will be grilled. With the water lapping over you and cooling your body as you swim along the surface, it is easy to underestimate how burnt you are getting.
- Stay out of the sun between midday and mid-afternoon. This is the period when UVA radiation is highest. If you are going ashore try to time it for after 1500.
- Some UVA penetrates cloud so even on overcast days there is a risk of UVA exposure and you should 'Slip, Slop, Slap'.

to keep the sprayhood up. Personally, I always fold the sprayhood down when approaching a harbour or an anchorage to give me good all-round visibility.

Tenders

These days, very few yachts have rigid tenders. Despite the fact that they are easier to row and perform better with an outboard, the advantages of inflatables outweigh the merits of a rigid tender. Some larger yachts still carry a rigid tender and some circumnavigators prefer aluminium dinghies (appropriately called 'tinnies' by Antipodeans), but for the most part, inflatables dominate the market as first choice for a tender.

There are a lot of inflatable manufacturers around, but few can compare with Avon. They cost more than many other makes but they do last. I have, in the past, opted for a cheaper well-known

It's worth investing some money in 'chaps' to protect the dinghy from UV degradation and bumps and scrapes on quays and jetties.

brand name, only to regret it. Avon (and a number of other manufacturers like Tinker Tramps in the UK, Apex in the USA, and Caribe in the Caribbean) use Hypalon, a rubber fabric made by Dupont, which is a lot tougher than the PVC materials used by most other manufacturers. Hypalon is more resistant to UV, petrol, oil and other substances. Most Hypalon is hand-glued whereas PVC can be machine-welded and although you would think that this produced a stronger bond, in practice it doesn't. Lots of manufacturers will call PVC by another name, but in the end PVC is just PVC and doesn't last like Hypalon.

There are other factors you need to consider in an inflatable apart from the construction and the material used. If you intend to row it, you will find that most of the models with a thole-pin attached to the oars that slots into a rubber or plastic block on the dinghy are next to useless. You cannot put any decent pressure on it and effectively are reduced to fluttering the oars up and down. Avon and a couple of other companies bond solid rubber rowlocks onto the dinghy and you can put a decent amount of pressure on these when rowing.

I labour the rowing point because although many people use an outboard for getting around, there will come a time when it won't start and you may need to row against a stiff breeze and choppy water. In most Mediterranean places you can easily row ashore – I probably use the outboard only half a dozen times in the season. Anyone who has used an outboard on a doughnut-type inflatable with a silly little bracket, added as an afterthought to the back, will know that inflatables with a rigid transom win hands down in the motoring stakes.

RIBs are a lot more common than they used to be, although for the Med their use is limited apart from a bit of posing at high speed. In most places you won't be commuting that far to the shore and unless you have davits or are going to tow it, a RIB is much heavier to haul up on deck. They also suffer badly in the rowing department, most of them being equipped with silly little rowlocks and oars that are not up to much. Further afield in the Tropics, where you may be anchored some distance offshore, a RIB makes a lot more sense.

There are a few additions you might want to make to the standard dinghy. Ultraviolet light degrades Hypalon and plays merry hell with PVC. Some people get canvas covers made up for the top of the dinghy to protect it from UV. If you carry the dinghy inflated on deck it is also a good idea to have a cover made to put over it during all those hours it sits there in the sun.

One last thing: a cheap umbrella is a useful bit of dinghy equipment for times when there is a bit of chop. Just put the umbrella up and point it forward and you have one of the best spray dodgers around. Sounds silly, but it works a treat.

Rigid tenders are rare these days and an inflatable with an outboard is the usual choice.

Swimming ladders and passerelles

Swimming ladders used to be tacked on as an afterthought, but bear in mind that this item of equipment will be in constant use in the hot Mediterranean summer. Many modern yachts with a sugar scoop, accessed via the aft end of the cockpit, are admirably set up with a decent swing-down ladder for swimming off the stern and a freshwater shower to wash off the salt after swimming. If you do not have this sort of arrangement then you need to think about sorting out something effective.

Most of the swimming ladders that hang over the topsides, usually amidships, are next to useless. Rope and folding plastic ladders are especially useless. You need a rigid ladder and, ideally, it should fold down off the transom. It must also have at least three rungs and preferably four. And the rungs should ideally have wooden treads on them so there is a wider area to support delicate feet.

Apart from the fact that the ladder will be essential for swimming, it is also an important piece of safety equipment for getting someone who has fallen overboard back on the boat. I have used the swimming ladder in earnest a couple of times in man overboard situations and a transom-hung swimming ladder does work well in this situation. You can usually position the boat so it is head-to-wind and waves and despite the fact that the transom is going up and down in the swell, with good timing you can grab someone and get them on board with just a bit of bruising and minimal panic.

The other item you are going to use a lot when berthed stern-to in the Mediterranean is a passerelle. Passerelles can be anything from an exquisite creation with safety lines, carpet and recessed lights to a basic plank with a hole in the end to tie it onto the boat. Yachts with a sugar scoop again have the advantage here as it is comparatively easy to arrange a passerelle leading off the scoop or higher up on the transom.

Whatever passerelle you decide on, whether a sophisticated design or the bog-standard plank, you will need somewhere to store it. A plank stored on the side-deck will get in the way so you may decide to spend some money on something a little more flashy. If you are cruising long term in the Mediterranean,

it is worth looking at some of the folding designs which stay in situ, folded up flat, and can be strapped to the transom. In the end, your choices come down to how deep you want to dig into your wallet and what sort of arrangement will be practical for the transom design on your boat.

For a yacht that normally berths bow-to you can buy ready-made ladders that hook over the pulpit, which have a brace with a padded V which rests on the bow. This overcomes the problem of hoisting your-self up and over a pulpit from low quays. On the first charter boats I took to the Mediterranean, the pulpit was designed with a U-section on the top to make getting on and off easy when bow-to and this can be incorporated into a new pulpit or possibly the old one can be modified.

Ventilation

Most yachts in the Mediterranean do not have adequate ventilation below decks. Ventilation is just as important when you are not living on the boat so that everything does not become damp and mouldy over the winter.

When the boat is winterised make sure that there are sufficient dorade vents and other ventilators to keep air moving through the boat. Locker doors should have a louvered grill, or can be left open. Bunk cushions should be propped upright and under-bunk lockers left ajar.

When you are on the boat you need a good through air flow to keep everyone comfortable down below. Traditionally, hatches open facing aft to avoid them being swept away by big waves. This

Here, a sturdy, custom-built stern passerelle, hung from a halyard, doubles up as a swimming ladder.

Good ventilation is essential for a comfortable night's sleep so make sure your boat has plenty of hatches.

comes from the days when hatches were custom-made in wood and I don't think it applies to modern aluminium hatches. If a wave is going to shear a hatch off, it's going to do it whichever way the hatch is facing. On *Skylax* and *seven tenth*s all the hatches open facing forward so that they scoop up air when at anchor; when there is any spray around I close them. It doesn't seem to matter which way they face since the spray always seems to curve precisely around and down inside anyway when sailing.

It's worth having canvas covers made for your hatches so you don't get a greenhouse effect below. Covered hatches will keep you a lot cooler below and the covers will also stop the perspex from crazing.

Apart from having as many dorade vents, hatches and opening ports as possible, life can be immeasurably better with the addition of a wind scoop. This simple device will funnel air down

below and can make it chilly at night even in midsummer. Most yachts use a wind scoop to direct air flow down the fore-hatch and out through the saloon or the main hatch. In addition to a wind scoop for the fore-hatch, I also have small wind scoops for the saloon hatches and mix and match the number of scoops in operation depending on the wind strength. At times you can have too much air movement below so it becomes uncomfortable.

Yachts with quarter-berth and aft cabins need to pay particular attention to air movement. For a traditional aft cabin it is easy enough to rig a small wind scoop, but for quarter-berth cabins this can be more difficult. Often there will only be a small opening port into the cockpit. I have seen a fabric dorade-type wind scoop made up to funnel air into an opening port in the cockpit for the quarter-berth cabin, but ideally you need a hatch, even a small one, on the cabin top where a normal wind scoop can be rigged. It is worth thinking hard about ventilation for quarter-berth cabins or you will find that they get impossibly hot in the Mediterranean summer to the point where no one wants to sleep there.

Few yachts in the Mediterranean have air conditioning installed and personally I think that is a good thing. There is nothing worse than being next to a boat in a harbour or anchorage that continually runs a generator to keep the air conditioning unit working. With good ventilation, and the addition of a couple of cheap wind scoops, you can be comfortable down below and avoid annoying everyone with a smelly and noisy generator.

WIND SCOOP DESIGN

My preferred design for a wind scoop is shown here. The commercially produced scoops can be used when at anchor, although they usually collapse as the boat swings round. The design shown below, although it has less area than the commercial scoops, will funnel more than enough air below and will keep doing so. When the boat swings at anchor, the adjacent panel will fill instead of the whole affair collapsing until the boat swings directly into the wind again. This design also has the benefit of working effectively in harbour, which conventional designs often fail to do unless the wind is blowing in exactly the right direction.

My preferred design for a wind scoop works whatever the relative wind direction is to the boat

Wooden crossbar folds for stowing

Insect screens

Whether to construct insect screens for your boat or not is a matter of choice. You will find that in many parts of the Mediterranean you will be relatively free from mosquitoes – which are the main pests. Personally, I do not use insect screens for a number of reasons. Firstly, you need to cover every single hatch, port and dorade vent inlet. You will need to put screens in place before sunset and once screens are in place you must leave them there. This is all so much of a chore that I don't bother. If you lift the screen from the main hatch to come or in or out, Sod's Law states that at least one hungry mosquito will get in while you are fiddling about with the screen. Unless you retire to bed or go below before sunset, screens are not all that useful. Screens also restrict the movement of air down below so the boat is not properly ventilated once the screens are in place.

Instead of screens you can use a repellent such as the 12V tablet gadget that plugs into a cigarette lighter point. You can buy these in many camping shops and they use the same tablets that the 220V versions use. These don't smell a lot, produce minimal heat or fug when the small element warms up to heat the tablet and mosquitoes hate them. One tablet will last the night and in yachts up to 40 feet or so you should only need one tablet. On *seven tenths* we used a mosquito net which is rigged from hooks screwed into the deckhead which works very well. This also has the advantage that you can keep a wind scoop rigged to funnel air down below.

A mosquito net rigged over the bed does away with the fuss of fitting screens over every opening hatch.

Refrigeration

There are few boats without refrigeration these days. While marine refrigeration units have improved dramatically in recent years, you may still find that a large chunk of your power goes on keeping the fridge cold and a large chunk of money can go towards maintaining the refrigeration unit. Before buying, bear in mind that there are a lot of models on the market that may work well in northern climes, but will not work well in the high ambient summer temperatures of the Mediterranean. There are a number of aspects to consider.

Thermo-electric coolers

These work using the Peltier effect, whereby an electric current applied to a semiconductor warms one side and cools the other. A fan wafts the air away from the hot side – the cool side is situated inside the fridge cabinet. These systems do not work well in the high summer temperatures of the Mediterranean and cannot be relied on for long-term refrigeration on board.

Dedicated fridge units

These are often AC/DC and can be bought as a stand-alone unit much like a mini-version of those you buy for a house. They are power-hungry and generally poorly insulated. They are also usually front-loading types so that every time you open the door, cold air falls out. They have the merit that when you are in harbour with shore-power you can plug them in to 220V.

Built-in 12V units

A compressor powered by the 12V (or 24V) boat batteries cools an evaporator or holding plate for a built-in icebox. This is the most common system for the Mediterranean and, depending on the installation, works well.

You need to have a well insulated (minimum 3 in/7.5cm) icebox with a sufficiently large evaporator or holding plate and an efficient way of removing heat from the compressor unit.

Built-in engine-run compressor

A compressor is run off the engine using an electromagnetic or other clutch to turn the compressor on and off. This system should use a holding plate in the icebox. This is the most efficient method but it does mean you need to run the engine for an hour in the morning and evening to keep the fridge cold; that can be exceedingly annoying to others in an anchorage or harbour. There are also hybrid systems which use the engine and 12V to run the compressor. Engine-run units are the most costly to buy.

Living without a fridge

I have cruised long distances without a fridge and, even now, I refuse to be dictated to by my fridge. I'm not going to go into a marina and hook-up to shore power or run the engine just to power the fridge. This is a madness inherited from our convenience-led lives and you can get by very well without a fridge or with minimal use of one. 'Cold beer on board', I hear you say. My answer is simply:'Do you know how good that first beer tastes in a bar on the beach after a long day at sea?' What I mean is that you really do taste it, savour it, once you have anchored and rowed ashore to get it. Wind down and take time to savour that frosting on the outside of the bottle and that wonderful, cool sensation of liquid amber trickling down your throat. Or a glass of white wine or cold orange juice – whatever appeals to you.

If you live without a fridge you will very soon become accustomed to shopping for your lunch or dinner on a daily basis and will take advantage of the wealth of fresh produce available; this is a market in Turkey.

Compared to the Tropics, the Mediterranean has relatively low humidity and this makes it a lot easier to keep vegetables and fruit fresh. A lot of people like the idea of hanging a net somewhere for storing vegetables and/or fruit, on the principle that the extra air circulation helps to keep them fresh. That's fine as long as the net doesn't crash around when you are sailing, and provided that you find the soggy tomato or orange in the middle before it oozes over whatever is below. Vegetables and fruit are better stored in a well-ventilated locker. Root vegetables can be wrapped in newspaper, which absorbs any moisture that might cause them to go off. Likewise, cabbages and lettuce can be wrapped in newspaper to stop moisture causing rot. Change the newspaper every few days or it will become soggy. Eggs can be kept in plastic egg containers with a small hole drilled in the top of each individual compartment to keep air circulating. This also makes it easy to turn the eggs every few days.

FRIDGE FACTS

- Most compressor units use a fan to move hot air away from the compressor unit, so you need to make sure that air can circulate freely around the unit and cooler air can get in. Some compressors are sea-water cooled, which is probably the most efficient system, if a little more complicated. A new design of unit, which cools the compressor by circulating water around the outlet for the galley sink, is reported to work well.

- For all 12V units you will need to have adequate battery power and some way of topping up the batteries at anchor. This usually involves solar panels or a wind generator. Although many manufacturers give normal operating loads at around 5–8 amps for a compressor, they do seem to eat up a lot more. In any case, the fridge will probably be working continuously throughout the day in the height of summer, so that means around 60 to 100 amps over a 24 hour period with some cycling off at night. That is a lot of juice so you will need some way of topping it up. In practice, most people tend not to have the fridge on all the time.

- Modern fridges use a refrigerant (commonly HFC134A) that does not contain CFCs which damage the environment. In many Mediterranean countries, you may only be able to get CFC refrigerants (commonly CFC-R12) so it is worth checking whether your system can handle both types of refrigerant; carry a couple of cans of HFC as well.

- If the system only has an evaporator plate then you can stack chemical cold-packs around it (the manufacturers have thought of a delightful miscellany of names: Eskimo, Penguin, Snowflake, Chemi-cold) to work like a sort of holding plate.

  The evaporator will cool the cold-packs down and they will keep cooling the fridge when the compressor is turned off.

- Some compressors, usually the engine-run type, can be used to keep a small freezer unit cold. I advise against having a combined freezer/fridge unit, as to keep the freezer cold you will have to run the engine. This means that you cannot leave the boat to go away for a day or two because you need to run the engine to keep frozen food from going off. And when the system has a hiccup (as they all regularly do) then there is a risk that all your frozen food will spoil.

- In many places you can get block ice or bags of ice cubes, which will help out ailing fridges in high summer temperatures. As a friend put it: 'ice is nice and freon is for peons'.

Cheese can be kept in oil. Vacuum-packed meats like bacon will keep up to 3–4 days as long as they are sealed. Salami and other cured meats keep a long time.

There are lots of ways of getting around the food cooling problem that are worth thinking about even if you have a fridge. You don't want to be a slave to it because you need to run the engine or plug in somewhere. Wander ashore for that cold beer and forgo cold butter for the Med alternative of bread dipped in spicy olive oil and tomato paste.

Holding tanks

The legal requirements for having a holding tank vary from port to port, let alone from country to country. And these regulations are changing by the day. Different regulations are in place for private and charter boats, foreign and home flag boats. Practically speaking, though, a holding tank of sufficient capacity to store black water for at least three days is now a necessity on a yacht based in the Mediterranean. The latest regulations for each country can usually be found in the relevant Pilot book or Almanac, or from the local marina. Many countries around the Mediterranean will fine you for dumping black water in a harbour or bay. Spain, France, Italy, Greece and Turkey all have laws with substantial fines for dumping black water close to the coast. This effectively means that unless you are going to sprint ashore all the time, you will need to have a holding tank. In some countries you can be fined for dumping grey water in a harbour or bay although this is rare.

In the future it is likely that more countries will require them so it is worth thinking about fitting a holding tank system to a yacht that does not have one. Even if a holding tank is not required by a particular country, you should still think about fitting one. Who wants to go swimming in an anchorage where yachts are discharging directly overboard and what gives you the right to pollute enclosed harbours? I can hear a chorus of: 'Why should we fit a holding tank when the local sewerage is discharged directly into the harbour or the sea?' The answer is simply that pleasure boats

should not add to the problem and, in any case, most countries are installing treatment plants and discharging less and less raw sewerage into the sea.

Pump-out stations are becoming more widespread, with facilities in most new marinas throughout the Mediterranean. Yachts should use this facility wherever possible, but your holding tank should also conform to MARPOL regulations, which require it to be pumped out three miles or more offshore. In the past, a lot of designs have used a Y-valve to divert waste from the outlet to a holding tank elsewhere in the boat which could then be pumped out when the Y-valve was opened. This is a complicated system requiring long pipe runs because the holding tank was often situated in the forepeak or the bilges in the saloon; a lot of plumbing for valves and breathers, and often a dedicated pump for the holding tank is needed. If the plumbing was less than perfect, a leak could develop leading to smelly consequences; often the holding tanks themselves could start to smell in hot weather.

Many boats now adopt the system whereby a holding tank is situated in the heads and the toilet pumps continuously through it to the outlet. The holding tank is utilised by closing the outlet seacock. Emptying the tank is simply a matter of opening the outlet seacock – gravity and a bit of pumping does the rest. The holding tank itself is best fabricated from polyethylene or GRP, which can be custom made to fit most spaces. Stainless steel tanks will often be eaten away by uric acid after 4–5 years. Most heads can accommodate at least a small holding tank although it should really be at least 50 litres, preferably bigger. One of the

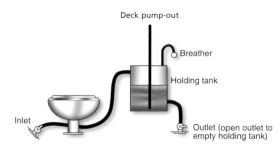

Simple holding tank system.

advantages of this system, apart from minimal piping runs, relative absence of valves and an additional pump, is that water is always flowing through it, so it is regularly flushed out. Incidentally, a litre bottle of Coca-Cola mixed with some fresh water is the ideal cleaning agent if left in the tank for a few hours.

One tip: do not put toilet paper down your loo; instead, put it in a small rubbish bin and dispose of it properly when ashore. It takes around 20-30 years for toilet paper to decompose on the sea bottom, but much less than this on land. Toilet paper is the most common culprit for blocking holding tanks. If you think about it, chopped up paper and water and a bit of dung makes a very good papier mâché, which will block pipes very easily. To clear a blocked pipe, use a dinghy pump to try to blow the blockage back up the pipe. Trying to force it further down the pipe usually only compresses the blockage more.

Power on board

Modern boats use a lot more amps than their predecessors of just a few years ago. Refrigerators are pretty much considered essential these days and chew up a lot of amps (see page 51). Navigation lights, interior lights, music systems, instruments, radios, laptop computers and mobile phone chargers, not to mention autopilots and electric anchor winches, all contribute to a total amp load that needs to be replaced one way or another. In many parts of the Mediterranean you will have to rely on generating power yourself rather than plugging in at a marina or harbour. The following points are a general guide to a much bigger subject that can easily fill a book of this size.

Battery capacity

Most boats will have a dual-bank battery system with one set of house batteries and an engine-starting battery. As a rule of thumb, your house battery capacity needs to be 3–4 times your estimated average daily consumption. If you work out the amount of time equipment is running and multiply it by its average consumption in amps, then you will get a figure in amp hours that you can work with to estimate battery consumption.

For example: a refrigerator used for 5 hours a day may consume 5 amps, which means that you will use 25 amp hours in a day. Other equipment may use something like 50 amp hours. You will then need a minimum battery capacity of 225 amp hours. Just remember to add in all sorts of things like the music system, navigation lights, anchor light, and so on. It will all be a bit of a guestimate, but at least you have something to go on; if in doubt, just add more battery capacity. On *seven tenths* (36 ft) I worked on something like 5 times my estimated consumption with house batteries giving 500 amp hours and the engine starting battery providing 200 amp hours. On *Skylax* we work on 380 amp hours for domestic, 150 amp hours for engine start and 150 amp hours for the anchor winch battery. We'll need to upgrade to at least 500 amp hours when the domestic batteries are getting to the end of their life. And I'm the Amp Miser incarnate.

Battery type

Basically, deep-cycle wet, gel, or dry batteries (also called AGM or Absorbed Glass Mat) all use sulphuric acid and lead plates. The only exception to this are nickel-cadmium batteries which are heavy and expensive, but a lot more reliable. Traditional lead-acid batteries are really now very old technology and are not very reliable. There are endless arguments between cruisers over the merits of different battery types, but I believe that modern charging methods and TLC over the winter will do more to prolong battery life than choosing one type over another. A badly maintained gel or dry battery will die before a well-maintained wet battery.

Alternators

The alternator on your engine will deliver more amps to your batteries than any other system apart from a large generator. It is worth specifying, or changing, to a larger alternator than the standard one normally supplied with an engine. Most engines will come with a 40–55 amp alternator and a standard regulator. Even quite small engines can usefully take a larger alternator and all engines can and should use a marine alternator regulator, which charges

your battery in a multi-stage process. The latter kit is not cheap but it will soon repay its cost in both providing additional amps and intelligently charging your batteries. On *Skylax* I have a 100 amp alternator fitted with a marine regulator which delivers a three-stage charge to the batteries.

Basically, normal car regulators will charge at, say, 50 amps until the battery warms up and charging is resisted. This means that after a short time, often as little as 10–15 minutes, your batteries could be getting as little as 5 amps or less. Smart regulators have a more sophisticated way of measuring temperature and resistance in the battery bank and will deliver more amps to your batteries than a standard regulator. It is worth thinking about this sort of system before you opt for solar panels and wind generators for the simple reason that an alternator with a smart charger can put in over half an hour what your solar panel may take a couple of days to do, assuming there are optimum conditions for it to work.

Battery charger

A good marine battery charger is useful if you intend to be on shore power even for as little as 10 per cent of the time. In a couple of days, batteries can be returned to peak charge and often you will be paying for electricity anyway in a marina. In the summer it is important that your charger has adequate ventilation around it as it will get quite hot. Don't just rely on a normal, cheap car battery charger; unlike a marine charger, it does not sense the battery state and you risk damaging your batteries.

Solar panels

I am all for alternative (and quiet) ways of getting amps – solar panels will do this. It is important to remember that you won't get a huge number of amps from solar panels and they should be regarded as a nice ecological back-up to nasty engines and alternators. On *Skylax* we have two flexible deck-mounted 38 watt panels which are not in an optimum position, but do provide some amps to top up the batteries. Most solar panels will give about 50 per cent of their wattage if aimed at the sun and 25 per cent if randomly orientated. As far as I am concerned, the solar panel more or less runs a fridge or autopilot, except, of course, on cloudy days.

Wind generators

Like solar panels, wind generators should be considered as a back-up. Unlike solar panels, a lot of wind generators produce noise pollution that can be exceedingly irritating. Both solar panels and wind generators need to have a regulator if there is not one built in.

Generators

I don't have a lot to say about generators because I don't like them. Whether in an anchorage or in harbour there is nothing more irritating than a nearby boat running its generator. Come on, who wants to remember the noise and fumes of rush hour traffic jams? Boats running a generator, whatever the size, should ensure that it is not annoying anyone in the vicinity. Quite often a generator will be left running while crew go out to dinner, apparently oblivious to the fact that neighbours are subjected to noise and fumes.

A lot of boats have an arch on the back to take solar panels, wind generator and frequently an array of aerials and the radar.

Spares and repairs

Spares for most marine equipment are now much easier to find throughout the Mediterranean than they were just 10 or so years ago. In all the EU countries dealerships for most European equipment can be found or ordered from a supplier. In some countries, such as Greece, it can be cheaper to buy a new engine from a number of well-known manufacturers than in the UK, and in other countries you will find most spares at reasonable cost. For countries on the southern side of the Mediterranean, spares will be harder to obtain, although from somewhere like Tunisia you can pop across to Malta or from Morocco to Gibraltar. (See also Appendix 1.)

If you keep your boat permanently in the Mediterranean, and fly out to it every summer, then small items can be carried in your luggage. As long as you are not struggling to carry an outboard or a refrigeration unit through customs then for 99 per cent of the time you will have no problem at all. Getting items shipped out to a country outside the EU can entail a lot of hassle and some expense. In many cases it is best to hire an agent to smooth the whole process and he will of course charge a fee (sometimes not insubstantial) as well as other official and non-official fees he may have had to pay. Often it is better to cross from somewhere like Turkey to Greece or Tunisia to Malta to pick up a piece of equipment rather than face the sometimes unequal battle of getting an item through customs and onto your boat.

Like the spares situation, getting repairs done is now much easier than in recent years. There are efficient boatyards all along the northern Mediterranean and in Turkey, Cyprus, Israel, Tunisia and Morocco. On *seventh tenths* I had new teak decks laid and an Awlgrip paint job. This was carried out in Turkey at considerably less cost than in northern Europe (around 30 per cent less) using imported sealant, glue and paint. Some boatyards will use the old-fashioned sledge and runners to haul you or maybe a crane with a jib-frame, but most yards are equipped with travel hoists and experienced personnel to run them. Even in the eastern Med you can now find a couple of 350-ton travel hoists for hauling superyachts as well as lots of 40- to 100-ton hoists.

Often I am asked where I base my boat in the winter. Do I have one yard I go back to all the time? The answer is simply 'no'. There are so many yards around that, unless you are over 15–20 metres, you can turn up somewhere and be fairly sure of getting hauled. Most yards can fit 'just one more' yacht in and consequently I use yards all over the Mediterranean from Spain to Turkey. While I do have a couple of favourite yards in odd places that I nearly always return to if I am in the area, I am not worried if it is full or the price is not right as there are lots of other yards nearby. Information on yards and the facilities available can be gleaned from the relevant pilot for the area or by word-of-mouth.

When you leave your pride and joy behind, remember to lock up securely and, if possible, get a cover made like this one. It not only protects the boat but also deters the opportunist thief from helping himself.

5 | Equipping Yourself

In Gibraltar, the Balearics, Malta and other harbours around the Mediterranean you can find disillusioned yachtsmen contemplating selling their yachts and everything in them to return to the life they fondly thought they had left behind. A large part of the problem is money, or rather the lack of it. It is a nightmare being broke in a foreign country, far from the benevolent arms of the community you once lived in, where the state (you hope) provides, and friends and family comfort you. What was a minor problem at home can take on the dimensions of a catastrophe in foreign parts: a doctor's bill, a repair job on the engine, a trip home to see an ailing parent, someone who owes you money and is mysteriously away when you call. Some can survive on very little; I know of one yachtsman who survived through a winter on potatoes and an egg or two, but for most of us things crop up that weaken and break the spirit unless we are in some way prepared for them.

But lack of money, and worse, the things you didn't budget for that erode both your bank balance and your morale, may only be part of the reason why not everybody fulfils the long planned-for dream. After all, many yachtsmen, not all of them young and fit men ready to turn their hand to anything, enjoy cruising around the Mediterranean on small budgets. A little forward planning to equip yourself for the voyage is just as important as equipping the boat.

Money

So you need it, but not as much as some think, if you are prepared to budget. If you have an expensive lifestyle at home and wish to take all the trappings with you then you must budget for that. Jot down what it costs to live for a month and add half again: Rémy Martin, Roses lime juice, stilton and *The Sunday Times* will all cost a lot more in the Med – when you can get them. But if you live like the locals, drink the regional wines, eat local sausages and goat's cheese and read a fifth-hand *Times* passed along from another yacht, then your living costs plummet dramatically. Economical living is all common sense, but there are many who fall by the wayside. Most of us are located somewhere between these two extremes.

Apart from your basic living costs you will need a fund for any contingency that may crop up: a shredded genoa, an engine on its last legs, a yard bill rather higher than you expected. Even if you have a brand spanking new yacht you will need this security fund; a figure that varies even more dramatically from person to person. I am quite happy to get my spending down to a figure that horrifies even my close friends. When money is in short supply I lower my expectations and living standards, keeping only enough in reserve to buy the basic necessities and the air fare to somewhere where I know I can get a job. Others have a sizeable nest egg and property that enables them to weather just about any disaster that might occur.

Cash machines

The simplest way of getting cash in the Mediterranean is to use ATMs, 'Automatic Teller Machines' or 'hole-in-the-walls' to most people. Using one of the major credit cards like Visa or MasterCard works nearly everywhere in the Mediterranean. It is rare, even in some out of the way places, not to find an ATM somewhere. Most of the major banks can arrange for you to have a debit card operating with your current account. This way, any money you withdraw at an ATM comes off your account straight away. Alternatively, you can have a true credit card where the amount stacks up until you pay it off. The only problem here is that all the banks give a poor rate of exchange: the 'tourist rate' and not the actual bank rate, for cash advances on a credit card. Most of them also charge a commission, usually a minimum amount plus a percentage on larger amounts. One way you can get around this is to open a Euro account with the bank or an account in a bank in somewhere like France, and get a cash/credit card for that account. You will still pay a charge for transferring money to that account, although at least you will get close to the bank rate and not the 'tourist rate'.

One other way to get cash is to use a prepaid card. Prepaid cards are usually under the Mastercard umbrella and allied to a UK bank or building society. You

Keep your costs down by eating out in simpler restaurants rather than fancy affairs with linen tablecloths and bossy waiters. Kale Koy in Turkey even has a pontoon to tie up to.

You can recognise a live-aboard boat from 50 paces. No laundromat costs, fitting out all done in-house, and I bet there is some home-made marmalade on the go down below.

load the card with Euros by transferring money from your bank account at an agreed rate, and it then allows you to spend the money up to the amount you have on the card, either by withdrawing cash or spending as you would normally with Mastercard. The exchange rate for cards like FairFX and Caxton is usually better than that of the major banks, they do not charge to transfer the money, and only a small fixed charge is made for cash withdrawals. It means that you can transfer funds at a known exchange rate, so you know exactly how much you are spending. You can reload the card easily using the internet or by phone. You do need to be careful of how much you load as the law regarding repayment of funds should the card company go bust is ambiguous to say the least.

Euros
The introduction of the euro has made things very easy for travelling in EU countries where your cash from one country can be used in any other EU country. Many of the other countries bordering the EU will also accept euros and it has effectively replaced the US dollar as the hard currency to carry as cash in the Mediterranean. For some of the Maghreb countries it may still be useful to carry US dollars, though in the near future the euro is likely to be as acceptable as the old greenback.

Credit cards
Most businesses will take the major credit cards for transactions and it is now common to pay marina and boatyard fees with a card. Likewise, most shops, such as large supermarkets and chandlers, will take cards. For small shops and local restaurants you will still of course have to pay in cash, but it is surprising how many places take plastic for even quite small transactions. Charge cards like American Express and Diners Club are less

frequently acceptable and you would be ill-advised to travel with just these cards.

Travellers cheques and money transfers

These days, hardly anyone carries travellers cheques although they could be handy as a backup. What you should avoid like the plague is having money cabled to a bank. This does not work well even in the EU where most of the major banks will take five working days to get money to another bank. In some places it can literally take weeks and I, and others, have frequently been frustrated by communications which have been 'lost' or funds that have been 'misplaced'. If at all possible, avoid transferring funds to an overseas bank.

Internet banking

Most of the major banks now offer internet banking and this is a great help. You can monitor your account, check for deposits and withdrawals, and arrange for direct debits and standing orders.

Half-an-hour in an internet café will be all you need to check things over and ensure you are on target with that budget, or establish that you will have to make contingency plans for extra funds. If your bank does not offer internet banking then it may be worthwhile changing to one that does or operating a 'Med account' with one of the virtual banks that has no high street presence.

CRUISING COSTS IN THE MEDITERRANEAN

Below are approximate, averaged, percentile break-downs of where the money goes when cruising. This is all a guestimate based on my costs and those of others and there is no way that it can accurately reflect everyone's expenditure. Really it is just there so you can go – gulp, does it cost that much for xyz?

Six months on board and six months laid up

Food and eating out	25%
Marina and harbour dues	10%
Maintenance and repairs	20%
Emergency fund	5%
Travel (back home & other)	8%
Fuel	3%
Communications	2%
Misc	2%
Entertainment	3.5%
Insurance (boat & self)	7.5%
Hauling and antifouling	14%

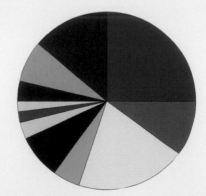

A proportional breakdown of cruising costs six months afloat and six months ashore.

It is a truism to say that how much you spend in these categories is dependent on how much you have to spend. Most cruisers without huge bank accounts spend their whole budget and usually a bit more. Below, I have worked out some cruising budget categories with general remarks on how it will work. The figures are for a couple cruising on a 38 foot yacht, which is about the average size for many cruising people. It is important to remember that the size of yacht will seriously affect your financial health. It is much easier to make ends meet on a 30-footer compared to a 50-footer. Take another look at the comparison figures in Chapter 2 for running yachts of differing sizes.

€1000 and under per month This is a budget where nothing is taken for granted. Berthing in a marina will be occasional and only in cheap marinas. The diet on board will be restrained and probably largely vegetarian for much of the time. Eating out ashore will be minimal. Everything on board will be self-maintained and no major new equipment can be purchased. Any calamity, an engine breakdown or a shredded sail, will wreck the budget. That said, I've managed on this amount and so have others.

€1400 per month The occasional berth in a marina. The diet on board will be more varied and you will be able to fund a modest drinks cabinet. Eating ashore will be possible, though care will be needed not to blow-out too often. Most repairs will be carried out by

the owner and any new equipment or major repairs must be carefully budgeted for.

€1700 per month You can visit a marina more often although care is still needed. The diet on board will be really quite good and a beer or two and a bottle of wine here and there are affordable. A run ashore for a meal or drinks is no problem although you need to watch it at times. Most repairs are still carried out by the owners, but getting things done ashore and some winter maintenance will not break the bank. New equipment and replacement gear is quite affordable although a major item like a new sail or outboard is going to stretch things.

€2000 per month You can afford marinas some of the time and if you get locked in by bad weather it is not a hassle. The diet on board is excellent and you can afford some good wines to go with a meal. Eating out ashore sometimes is part of the deal. There will be some onboard maintenance and some by professionals. A new engine or suit of sails is possible although you will probably have to economise for a while afterwards.

€2500+ per month Life is sweet, but you still need to watch it on modifications to the boat.

One last thing to remember is that the joy you get out of the cruising life is in no way related to your budget. Just look at some of those miserable faces on the superyachts.

Funding

If you have 'loadsa-money' you can skip this section. Most of us don't have endless funds and need to finance our cruising in some way.

Pensions and investment incomes

If you have a pension or an income from investments then it is really just a matter of living within those boundaries. I should emphasise again that a lot of people sustain their cruising on comparatively modest budgets and do not have huge incomes derived from private pensions or investment funds. I'm not an accountant so I won't go into the vagaries of the economics of investments or different pension schemes, except to say that all the indicators are pretty bleak with lots of pension funds reneging on predicted pay-outs. All advertisements for investments of any type carry the warning that 'funds can go down as well as up' and if your investment earnings do go down then you are going to have to cruise on less.

If you control a share portfolio yourself, then it is perfectly possible to buy and sell via the internet. There are plenty of reliable internet brokers and share prices are now relayed to the internet with a much shorter delay from the postings in the market. Anybody doing this will need to be able to access the internet from on board and this is a lot cheaper to do now than in years past. Most people doing this use a dedicated 3G data card utilising the local network of whatever country you are in. Nor do you have the same sort of access to data and the informal contacts you have at home. The upside of this is that you

You will need to have a reasonable contingency fund for unexpected problems like rigging, sail, or engine troubles.

could be buying and selling at anchor in a wonderful bay, and after a busy morning trading you can just dive over the side to wash away the market blues.

Any income from a fixed pension or investment can simply be paid into a home account and funds obtained using your credit/debit prepaid card. There is really no point in trying to sort out something more complicated as it can, and often will, go wrong.

Savings

This is the ultra-safe option, although in recent years it has not provided much of an income. If bank rates are high you can stick your savings in a high interest account and live off the interest. You need a big chunk of capital and in real terms your capital diminishes with inflation if you live off the interest.

Renting out your home

A lot of people move on board and rent out their home. There are a number of things to think about if you are contemplating doing this:

- Short-term lets of six months are possible, but most agents want to rent a property for at least a year, preferably with the possibility of renewal after that. Most letting agents use a standard short-term tenancy agreement which runs for six months, but will rarely let for less than one year. In addition, remember that you are going to have to store a lot of your personal items and this may cause inconvenience and expense if the items are in commercial storage.
- While it is perfectly possible to let the

The more you can repair yourself the less you will have to pay others. Some cruisers set themselves up to make a bit of money from work like sail repairs.

property yourself, it makes sense to use an agent. Agents are best found by personal recommendation. Make sure they have been in business for a while and preferably belong to a professional association like ARLA, the Association of Residential Letting Agents.

- Agents charge various levels of fees depending on the service offered. An 8–10 per cent fee is common for a basic letting service which will include marketing a property, finding and vetting a suitable tenant, obtaining references and preparing a tenancy agreement and inventory. A 15–18 per cent fee will be charged for a managed letting service where they collect the rent monies, pay bills, regularly inspect the property, and oversee any necessary maintenance work. It is also worthwhile taking out insurance to cover any rent not paid and this could be anything from 1–4 per cent of the rent. Quite possibly you will have to deduct 20 per cent of your estimated

Don't be tempted to take short cuts for income! This yacht was impounded for drug smuggling in Greece and the skipper and crew earned themselves a long stretch in jail.

rent from a property to pay agents fees and any maintenance on the property.

- In the end you will probably not find tenants that will look after the property in the way you want. You need to accept that there will be some damage to your pride and joy and it will not be in the same state you left it in when you set off cruising.

A steady trade

It is possible to find work in the Mediterranean with just a willing pair of hands, but it is easier if you have a 'steady trade' (to borrow a phrase from the late Tristan Jones) or a profession. Of the professions, only doctors, dentists and engineers find employment easily. Lawyers, teachers, middle management executives, town planners and anybody else who falls under those much misused terms 'professional' or 'executive' will find it extremely difficult to find work away from home.

A steady trade is the thing to have, especially if it has anything to do with yachts. If you are a proficient marine engineer (I mean engines), know about marine electrics or electronics, a rigger, boat carpenter, GRP specialist, welder or sailmaker, then you will invariably find work from other yachtsmen or charter fleet operators. These days most cruising yachts will have at least one computer on board, often running vital navigation software as well as being the mainstay for email communications, photo storage and onboard entertainment. If you are a trained computer hardware or software engineer you will likely find abundant work. The tricky bit is to make it pay. As in so many other fields, a ticket stating a certain degree of competency can mean nothing, while a job well done or a word of mouth recommendation from another yachtsman can mean as much work as you can handle. The cruising community soon sorts out the charlatans from proper craftsmen,

If you are skilled at boat jobs, fixing engines is a particularly good one, then you should be able to find work once you establish a reputation as a reliable worker.

whether the latter have tickets or not.

Whether you have a trade or simply a willing pair of hands that can scrape and wield a paintbrush, do not expect to arrive somewhere and find work the next day. There will be a period in which you will find little or none at all until word gets around that you are looking for gainful employment and you are a reliable worker. A number of friends lived by settling down in an area and working through the winter and then cruising locally in the summer. One of the advantages of a cruising home is that you can take it with you to seek work elsewhere.

One alternative worth thinking about is working as a skipper or mate on a charter yacht for a limited period. Many of the larger charter companies require freelance skippers for inexperienced charterers but, as with any job,

you will need to check out the local employment regulations. Another line of work is delivering yachts in and out of the Mediterranean, a job that gives you a lot of freedom, but often imposes punishing deadlines. After a friend of mine was drowned en route from Britain to the Mediterranean because, I believe, the delivery deadline forced him to leave in weather he normally would have avoided, I stopped doing deliveries that leave little or no margin for bad weather. After all, it is your life out there and if you would not leave in your own yacht, why should you do it in someone else's?

Chartering your own yacht

Many people spend a lot of money building or buying a yacht in the belief that they will be able to charter it for three months or so of the year and have the rest of the time to themselves. There are many reasons why you cannot do this and some why you should not.

Around the Mediterranean various countries have different regulations for chartering a yacht. This applies to countries inside as well as outside the EU because, as yet, there is no single EU ruling on charter regulations. Although you can charter your yacht in most of the EU countries, to do so you must conform to the charter regulations of that country. This will often involve getting the boat surveyed to ensure it conforms to structural requirements (usually covered by a CE mark if applicable) and to safety regulations. For the latter you will need the requisite number of life jackets, an in-date life raft of sufficient capacity, flares and other safety equipment. This usually involves

Some make a living doing things they like.

contacting the relevant government department and obtaining the survey and certificates. In addition you will need to have certain qualifications for yourself and for crew depending on the size of the yacht. In the EU most countries will require you to add VAT to your charter fee and will want proof of payment.

To get up-to-date information on charter regulations you will need to make enquiries to the relevant authorities or an agency in the country you intend to charter in. Probably the best thing to do is to glean information from companies that already charter in that country. They will know how things work in practice and how long it takes to get any relevant authorisation to charter there.

People do charter illegally in Mediterranean countries by simply describing their paying guests as non-paying friends or crew. But you would be foolish to think that the authorities do not know about this, and some of the silly regulations introduced recently in some countries (Greece springs to mind) are a direct result of such illegal

chartering. It muddies the waters for people who are innocently cruising around and complicates life for us all. If you get caught you have no one to blame except yourself, and any moaning about the penalties (which can be large and might include a charge on the yacht involved) is misplaced, because those who do charter illegally know the risks they take and should be prepared to pay up if they get caught.

One legal loophole that some charter yacht owners use is to pick up passengers in one country and clear for another country. For instance you might pick up charterers in Italy and clear for Greece, but if you are doing this from the same place every two weeks or so, officials will inevitably realise what is going on and although they cannot stop you, they will find reasons to make life uncomfortable.

Assuming you have arranged to charter somewhere, then you must find clients, and there is an increasing number of charter boats chasing a limited market. A single yacht owner is at a disadvantage against the big charter companies who can afford to run an office and advertise extensively, and for this reason I would advise you to think hard about chartering your own boat for an income. It is a full time occupation, not something you can dabble your toes in and come out refreshed.

Tourism

In many places there are seasonal jobs going in the tourist industry. This can be anything from working in a bar or restaurant, to working as a courier or in a travel agency. In a lot of cases you will be working illegally and it is important to weigh up the cash coming in with the absence of any rights should it all go wrong. Try to get your wages paid on a weekly basis and be wary of excuses for not paying. Too often, illegal workers will be waiting for their pay for months and then find that, surprise, surprise, there is nothing legal they can do to get their money.

Writing

Money for nothing with some kudos thrown in as well, you might think. Writing articles and the odd book or two on board would seem to be the obvious way to earn money while cruising. The trouble is that everyone wants to do it, so magazine editors and book publishers are besieged by would-be writers. There are only so many articles a magazine can publish on sailing in the Mediterranean and few magazines out there that want to publish them. Work it out for yourself – it soon becomes apparent that there is not that much of a market out there. The same applies to books about sailing or about the Mediterranean; again there are only so many books that can be written and only a few publishers to take them on.

Before you get really carried away it is worth looking at the fees that are paid for articles. A national UK sailing magazine will pay around £100 per page for text and photos. Those photos have to be of good quality, usually 6 megapixel digital (or better) photos, which give a better reproduction, and there have to be enough of them to enable the editor to make a good selection. Photos are all-important as far as magazine editors are concerned, and if you do not have good photos to go with an article then the

chances are it will not be published.

If you are contemplating writing a book on sailing then you will be investing a large amount of effort and time for a comparatively small royalty cheque every six months. Granted you may have a bestseller hidden away in the left-hand side of the cortex, but normally specialist books sell in hundreds not thousands. Average hardback sales for a first book are usually of the order of 1500–2000. A typical contract will be for 10 per cent of the publisher's receipts from the cover price (ie after excluding discounts by the publisher, overseas sales, home distributors and other expenses). Unless you really like putting words together, don't do it or you are likely to disappoint both yourself and the publisher. Also, don't do it for the money because most writers don't make a lot – they just enjoy writing.

Insurance

Medical insurance

Falling ill abroad can cost you a lot of money and may become one of those catastrophes that exhausts your finances and breaks your spirit if you do not have insurance. In the Mediterranean, a modest cover of around £500,000–£1,000,000 for medical expenses and £500,000 for an air ambulance can be obtained quite reasonably. Typically, an annual multi-trip policy, with up to 3 months away from your resident country, will cost around £130–£150. Policies for shorter times away are much cheaper. For longer periods away premiums increase substantially, although you should find that an annual policy for the Mediterranean works out at around £600–£800 depending on age and other conditions.

Travellers from EU countries can get urgent treatment free or at a reduced cost, under a reciprocal health care agreement between EEA countries. (The EEA or European Economic Area comprises all the EU countries plus Iceland, Liechtenstein and Norway.) The old paper form E111 has been replaced with the European Health Insurance Card (EHIC). Application forms are stamped and processed by the post office and the new credit card sized official-looking EHIC (valid for five years) will be sent to you. This entitles you to free or reduced costs for medical treatment throughout the EEA and Switzerland. If you have to pay any charges, keep the receipts and apply at the local health authority for a refund. For prescriptions, show your EHIC to the pharmacist: some medicines are free; some have a non-refundable fee. The EHIC does not usually afford discounts for private healthcare. For more information, see the Department of Health website www.dh.gov.uk. Some countries, such as Gibraltar and Croatia, have reciprocal medical agreements with the United Kingdom so that you get free or cheaper medical treatment.

Remember that medical insurance and reciprocal medical agreements (EU or others) do not normally cover previously existing illnesses, nor do they cover pregnancy, abortion, nervous disorders, dentistry or cosmetic surgery. In some countries, particularly in North Africa, you will find that doctors want to give you the works: vitamin courses, wide spectrum antibiotics, suppositories,

anything they think they can prescribe in order to claim as much as possible from the insurers. Some judicious bargaining is in order here.

On the subject of doctors I will say that contrary to some opinion, medical treatment is good throughout Europe including Italy, Greece and Cyprus. In Croatia and Turkey medical treatment is good in the large cities and in large tourist resorts. There are also significant numbers of private hospitals around these days which should take you in with health insurance. Some countries (Greece and Turkey come to mind) now have a good reputation for quality private dental work that would be unaffordable in the UK. In Northern Africa medical resources vary dramatically between city and village.

Boat insurance

Insurance for a yacht in the Med is only a little more expensive than insurance in home waters; normally the rate is between one and one and a half per cent of the total value of the boat for a fully comprehensive cover. This is not an excessive amount for your home and means of transport. There are insurance firms in the Mediterranean countries that will insure your yacht, but some caution is needed here and if you have a good marine insurance broker at home then stick with him.

Nearly all insurance policies for the Mediterranean cover everything west of 34°E and exclude anything east of that. The excluded area includes the trouble spots of the Middle East: Cyprus, Syria, Lebanon and Israel. It also includes part of the non-troubled Anatolian coast of

Turkey and cover for this area if you are going there involves an extra premium. Depending on your insurer, you may be able to negotiate to include Anatolian Turkey and Cyprus under the normal cover.

Warranties

Much of the equipment you buy is covered by a warranty in the country you bought it in, but once you leave you may as well be on the Moon as far as many manufacturers are concerned. Check to see if a warranty will be honoured after you have left. Whether it will be or not, see if you can get the manufacturer's handbook for the equipment you have on board. Often you can repair equipment yourself – or at least give someone else a fighting chance – if you have the manufacturer's handbook, but remember that unauthorised repairs will in most cases invalidate warranty agreements.

Documentation

Personal documents

All crew on board need valid passports. Holders of EU passports do not need visas for EU countries and for most other Mediterranean countries a visa can be obtained at the port of entry if required. Holders of US and other passports can usually obtain a visa at the port of entry to most Mediterranean countries if required to do so. Only Libya and Algeria require a visa obtained in advance.

Many countries now require the skipper of a visiting yacht to produce proof of competence. The RYA Coastal Skipper or Yachtmaster qualifications are accepted everywhere. You can also obtain an RYA International Certificate of Competence (ICC) on application if you hold a Coastal Skipper or Yachtmaster qualification, or if the application form is signed by an RYA Yachtmaster instructor. Someone on board should also hold a radio licence (Short Range Certificate for DSC VHF and Long Range Certificate for SSB radio).

Boat documents

Registration papers for the yacht are required everywhere. They will need to state the name, home port, length, and registration number.

Part I is a continuation of the traditional Register of British Ships and used to be contained in a blue hardback cover known as the 'blue book'. Nowadays it is a laminated certificate which must be renewed every five years. It is acceptable everywhere.

Part II is a Register of Fishing Vessels.

Part III is the Small Ships Register (SSR) which was originally set up under the 1983 Merchant Shipping Act in response to the demand for a cheap and simple means of registering a yacht to sail abroad. From 1983 to 1991 the Small Ships Register was managed by the RYA. From 1991 to 1996 it was managed by the DVLA at Swansea and since 1996 by the Registrar General at Cardiff. See https://mcga.gov.uk/ssr

The authorities in many countries now ask for the insurance papers for a yacht. These papers must show a minimum of one million euros third party cover. In a number of countries you are required to

Most of the countries around the Mediterranean now run fast Coastguard boats to check on illegal cargoes of all descriptions, so you will most likely be checked somewhere *en route* through the Med.

have a translation of the insurance cover and specifically the third party cover in the language of that country. At the moment Spain, Italy and Greece demand you show this translation although in the future other countries may also require a translation. Some countries such as Greece also ask for specific cover for things like pollution clean-ups.

Occasionally, you will be asked for documentation such as the ship's radio licence, life raft certificate, the ship's log and, under the new SOLAS regulations, adequate charts and pilots along with a passage plan.

For European inland waterways you will require an endorsement for inland waterways on your ICC and a copy of CEVNI rules. Contact the RYA (website www.rya.org.uk) for further information on boat and personal documentation.

Keeping in touch

Snail mail
Although seemingly eclipsed by e-mail and mobile phones, this is still used by some cruisers. You can use *poste restante* at the main post office of most large towns and cities around the Mediterranean and, by and large, it works well. The drawbacks of sending mail are several: you are tied to a certain place at a certain time; in some countries mail is sent back after a short time (commonly 2–3 weeks) and owing to the vagaries of the weather you may arrive just after your mail has been returned. Even if your mail is there, getting it out of the clutches of the PO is not always straightforward. Always check under your first name, your yacht's name, and 'Esquire', as well as your surname.

If at all possible, get your mail sent to a private address such as a marina, yacht club, boatyard, or any other contact address you have, and make sure all mail is marked 'PLEASE HOLD'. Yachtsman's pilots or Almanacs for the Mediterranean usually have some useful addresses for mail. American Express offices also hold mail for cardholders but will not accept packages.

If you need to have packages sent out at short notice, then a courier company is the safest way. Most of the countries on the northern side of the Mediterranean now have courier offices in towns and cities and even some smaller resorts. In some places it is worth remembering that while the courier company guarantees three days or so, what they often mean is three days to a main city. A package may then be put on the bus or a ferry to get to where you are and this can take longer than the time it takes to get to that country.

Telephone and fax

With the exception of some of the Maghreb countries on the southern side of the Mediterranean, most countries have well-developed public telephone and fax facilities. Depending on your location, you can use a phonecard or credit card and, less commonly, coins to make calls. Fax facilities can often be found in stationers or offices, where a charge will be made for sending and receiving faxes.

Mobile phone

Digital cellular phones with GSM (Global System for Mobile Communications) capacity work in most of the countries around the Mediterranean. Your own service provider will need to have an agreement with the main service providers in a particular country. In practice, the system is seamless and your phone will register with a provider in a country when you turn it on. Most phones will automatically register, although at times it is worth manually changing provider where your phone 'sticks' on one provider even though the given signal is weaker than a rival's signal.

It is worth knowing that you pay for the cost of the signal into and out of your service provider's country. For a UK service provider, you pay the cost of the call both to and from the UK plus around 20 per cent on top. The person you are calling or who calls you will only pay for the point-to-point call in the UK. This means that using a UK phone costs more than you think, whatever your provider tells you. If you are going to spend much time in a particular country, it is worth getting a local SIM card for your phone with a local number on a pre-pay card system. You can then ask people to phone you on the local mobile number rather than your home country mobile, where the call is costing you a lot of money. Note that your handset will need to be unlocked before it will accept a different SIM card.

Note: EU regulations have put a limit on incoming and outgoing call charges in all countries. At present this is 35p per minute for outgoing calls and 15p per minute for receiving calls. Lower limits are planned in the future. Excellent news!

Voice Over Internet Protocol (VOIP)

Using a laptop with a broadband connection and a simple headset, many people are using VOIP to make telephone calls. To use the service, you need to subscribe to a VOIP provider, and set up an account and username. Call charges are a fraction of those incurred using a GSM phone, and calls between subscribers of the same provider are free. The only downside for travellers is the need to be connected to a broadband network. Skype is probably the best-known provider, although there are now many companies offering similar services.

E-mail

There are a number of ways of sending and receiving e-mail while cruising. The following assumes that you are familiar with Microsoft Outlook; it is also useful to be able to access your e-mail through the mail server's own webmail facility (such as via Yahoo, Gmail or Hotmail). The following is a brief round up of ways and means of doing so:

- **Smart phone and data communications** Most of the Mediterranean has an excellent 3G and GSM network which means you get a decent signal on your mobile phone almost anywhere, including out sailing some distance off the coast.

  Many people now use smart phones with call and data packages arranged with their UK provider that can be used for calls, email, social networking and internet browsing. Most people are unaware of their data usage as

they stream videos from Youtube, BBC iPlayer or similar, play online games, or tweet and post on social networks. When roaming on foreign networks you will need to be.

EU rulings have forced mobile phone companies to reduce their roaming call and data rates, although costs are still considerably higher than at home – your home allowances will not work abroad.

Provided your phone is unlocked for using abroad it will automatically pick up the local signal, which if 3G will mean data as well. You may want to disable data roaming until you know the costs as many smart phone applications are set to update automatically and can run up huge roaming charges that you are unaware of. Some providers allow you to prepay for roaming packages, both calls and data, which allow you to control your budget. Even if you have bought a data add-on remember that many apps use up sizeable chunks of your data allowance running in the background. Turn off any that you do not need, and consider using wi-fi to update stuff when you are in a café.

A 'roaming' EU data add-on to your existing phone contract costs around £10 a month, with a reasonable download limit for emails and light internet use. Check with your provider as roaming data charges vary enormously, and without an agreement it is possible to run up huge bills. Once it is all set up, you have all the convenience of receiving email, or checking weather forecasts wherever you are, and with some packages you can use your phone as a modem so you can use your laptop.

■ **Local Data SIM Card** In the same way as you buy a local pay-as-you-go SIM card for making calls, you can also buy a device for accessing the internet from your computer. The easiest way of doing this is to get a card and a data 'dongle' which plugs into the USB socket on your computer. This way you can access the internet using 3G or 4G networks where available, at local prices. Dongles and cards are available from most of the main mobile network retailers, and in most major tourist towns you will find a sales person who can explain the setup to you. Prices and data limits vary, and it is worth shopping around before you choose which network to go with. Other cruisers are a good source of info on the vagaries of the different options.

■ **Wireless Internet Access (Wi-Fi)** using a laptop computer or PDA Wi-Fi is a generic term used here to describe all wireless networks. Many marinas, hotels, cafés, bars, libraries and internet cafés are installing Wi-Fi networks, some of which are provided free of charge, or unsecured, while others require a password. Subscribers may pay a one-off connection charge and/or pay-as-you-go for x minutes', hours' or days' online access. Costs are reasonable for a fast connection, and you don't run up unseen bills on your GSM phone. Most new laptops have built-in wireless modems and will search automatically for available Wi-Fi networks. All you need to do is identify which network you wish to connect to. Older laptops will need to have a PCMIA card or USB dongle modem installed, but work in much the same way. Once connected, you can use your own mail portal such as MS Outlook, use a webmail facility, and of course access the internet with very fast broadband connections.

It is likely that Wi-Fi technology will continue to develop, and will probably become the standard method for accessing the internet using phones, PDAs, handheld computers and laptops.

■ **Internet cafés** Many quite small places have an internet café these days and if you have an internet webmail provider then it takes little time to download and send mail using a CD-ROM or memory stick if you need to save stuff. If you do not have a laptop to compile mail on and download it from the computer in the café then most places will let you print out the mail for a small fee. Costs are usually low and of course connection rates are fast, with many places on broadband or ADSL. As mentioned above, many internet cafés also have a Wi-Fi network, or a cable network to which you can connect using your laptop.

■ **INMARSAT or Iridium** Using these satellite systems, you can send and receive e-mail just about anywhere in the world.

INMARSAT transmissions vary depending on the system used. INMARSAT Fleet services offer fast enough speeds for video conferencing, but are also the most expensive and biggest of the range. Most others support transmission rates of 9.6

Kbps. The costs of the systems and transmission charges can be expensive, typically US$2–6 a minute.

- **HF Radio** There are a number of companies who will transmit data via HF radio including SailMail, Pinoak, GlobeEmail and the Ham Radio Network. Data rates are slow, typically less than 2.4 Kbps, but the service is relatively inexpensive. Annual contracts cost around US$250 and e-mails are free to send and receive.
- **Other means** There are a number of other methods of sending and receiving e-mail, although less common than those given above. A number of satellite phones are on the market that can transmit data. The most common is the resurrected Iridium (9.6 K), the new Inmarsat dedicated satphone, Thuraya, and Globalstar (9.6 K).

Guns and the non-combatant

Very few yachts in the Mediterranean carry firearms and there are good reasons not to do so. All countries around the Mediterranean demand that you declare any firearms on board and these will either be taken into bond by customs or sealed on board. Not declaring a firearm is just plain silly and the consequences in most countries are a prison term and the possible confiscation of your boat if you are caught.

Piracy in the Mediterranean is not very common and most countries take any incipient piracy seriously. There have been a couple of incidents around Albania and Italy in recent years, but the chances of

being relieved of your valuables are much less than in the UK. In recent years there has also been a high incidence of smuggling immigrants into EU countries, but this has involved only charter companies where a boat has been chartered and then sailed to somewhere like Turkey or Morocco to pick up illegal immigrants and ferry them across to an EU country.

There is no place for a gun on my yacht and I believe that if you are cruising in the Mediterranean (and elsewhere for that matter) you do not need to carry firearms. Put it this way: do you think you are capable of pointing a gun at another person and pulling the trigger to kill him if necessary? Most of us do not possess that instinct. In serious incidents it is likely he will be armed and more conversant with the theory and practice of killing. If you should be boarded by armed marauders, my advice is to give them everything they want and the likely outcome is that they will depart leaving you with your most precious possession – your life. I should add here that during more than 25 years cruising in the Mediterranean and other known pirate zones like the Gulf of Aden and Southeast Asia, there has never been even a hint of a threat.

If you feel you do need a deterrent against a low level threat then I would suggest that a baseball bat and a mini spray can of pepper or mace will do the trick. I carry both on board but have not even thought of deploying them. In addition, if you have a Very pistol on board then I'd suggest that an unarmed intruder would think twice when confronted with that large barrel. On a practical level the accuracy is probably in the region of 15 feet if you are lucky.

6 Navigating Around the Inland Sea

When I first sailed *Roulette* to the Mediterranean I was woefully under-equipped even for the 1970s. On board was a grid-bearing main compass, a hand-bearing compass, a lead-line and charts and pilots. You might think I was being irresponsible and maybe I was, but I did take *Roulette* safely from the UK to Greece when some better equipped yachts did not make it. Over the years, the development of navigation instruments and techniques has changed out of all recognition and now all of us have LCD displays lighting up the navigation area and in the cockpit. Through this lightning-fast evolution, from an EP of doubtful value to a GPS position to two or three decimal places, I always remember the advice from a well-travelled Frenchman I met who told me to 'always use my nose'. Whether you are arriving somewhere for the first or the twentieth time, it is vital that you sniff out the situation and look around you. The best equipment for navigation is not the hardware down below and in the cockpit, but the 'wetware' between your ears. It can perform incredibly complicated algorithms from diverse data and will frequently be the only thing keeping you safe when the digital readout says everything is apparently fine. Too often, yachtsmen charge on blithely past dangers to navigation and towards a new

harbour, trusting implicitly that the LCD readout will take them safely there when, in actual fact, they should slow down, stop and look around, and then proceed cautiously using *le nez* to sniff out dangers and act accordingly if it doesn't feel right.

I remember coming into Port Sudan one night after beating to windward for about 600 miles. My crew positively identified the red and green entrance lights to the harbour, but for me something didn't feel right. There was a near mutiny when I said we should wait until dawn. In the morning light it turned out the flashing red light marked a wreck on the reef, the actual port-hand entrance light was not working, and if we had continued on we would have run straight up onto the reef.

GPS

To encounter a cruising yacht without GPS is a rarity these days. GPS has revolutionised cruising and the old adage that if it breaks down, a yacht is left defenceless is pretty much ruled out by the cheapness of handheld sets; so that a backup GPS, even a couple, are carried on lots of yachts. And yet the ubiquitous GPS, and the very accuracy of the digital readout, carries significant dangers with it. An over-reliance on GPS and waypoints can lead yachts into disaster and is doing so with increasing frequency. Why should we get excited about old-fashioned navigation and pilotage skills when the GPS shows our position to two decimal places, tells us what course to steer and how far off course we are, and even guides the yacht over an electronic chart? Such complacency leads down the slippery slope to the jagged edge of a reef just under the water.

Waypoints

We all do it: plug in a waypoint and away we go. It's easy to forget that a waypoint has an origin and that origin is all-important.

■ The datum of a waypoint is critical. Most GPS receivers default to WGS84, which will eventually become the standard datum for all hydrographic departments worldwide. If possible you should check the datum of any waypoints you have and make the necessary corrections where they are known.

■ Often you will be given waypoints by other cruisers and here it is useful to know where the waypoint was taken. Was it at anchor in a bay, berthed in a harbour, at the entrance, or off an entrance point where the cruiser cut the corner? It could be critical in poor visibility or at night, or it may be that a waypoint was taken literally metres away from a reef or rock.

■ If you take waypoints off a chart or plug them in automatically onto an electronic chart you may find there is a discrepancy between the charted

position and the actual GPS position. See the comments on chart accuracy that follow in the next section.

■ If you are entering waypoints manually, double-check to make sure you have not made mistakes. The Cruise missile that hit a hospital in Afghanistan was the result of the operator getting the minutes the wrong way round when entering the position. As the old computer maxim goes: rubbish in, rubbish out.

■ Make a rough check on a chart of any received waypoints from whatever source to avoid entering someone else's errors. In my pilots there are literally thousands of waypoints and by my own hand, or with the help of publishing gremlins, errors do creep in.

Accuracy

Using GPS you can currently get an accuracy of around ±10 metres although repeated accuracy tends to give a higher figure than this and in some tests over a 24 hour period, errors have been greater than ±200 metres. In Europe SDGPS uses EGNOS satellites to give an accuracy of ±10 metres. I won't dwell on the pluses and minuses of receivers and the increasing accuracy of GPS and derivative systems because, for yachtsmen, this increased accuracy is to a large extent a red herring. While we can know our position to ±5 metres, we do not have charts accurate enough to plot these positions on.

How accurate is your chart?

Most charts for the Mediterranean were surveyed in the 19th century using astro-nomical methods to determine positions

We use all the usual electronic goodies on board, including laptop navigation and routeing programmes and a chart plotter when underway, but there is no substitute for old-fashioned research with a chart and pilot to familiarise yourself with an area. And there is no better substitute when the electronics all fail.

and old-fashioned triangulation surveying to get the shape of things. Many of these charts used obscure datum sources and in many cases the datum is not known at all. The charts are a triumph over the method with often outstanding accuracy in the face of adversity. Admiral Beaufort was shot and dangerously wounded in Turkey while surveying. Nelson surveyed places like La Maddalena on the north of Sardinia while hunting Napoleon. Over the years these surveys have been updated and improved upon, but it is important to remember that most of the original surveying for the charts we use was carried out in the 19th century. Most modern surveying touches upon bits of coast or around commercial harbours and covers very little of the blue and green stuff we sail upon.

To get charts more in line with WGS84 has meant shifting the lat and long lines on the chart, and this is a practice fraught with dangers. By just moving the lat and long lines, no account is taken of discrepancies between actual position according to WGS84 and any original cartographic errors. What is needed is for the world to be resurveyed using satellite pictures so charts agree exactly with WGS84 datum; but in this cash-strapped world where the 'market forces' determine most of what happens, this is unlikely and we are left with our 19th-century charts rejigged to agree with WGS84 as well as possible.

The discrepancies between a GPS position and the charts that the positions are plotted on is best seen with electronic charts. Many people imagine that the

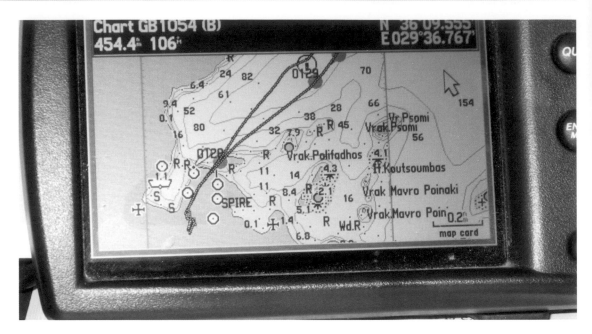

The basic surveys for all the charts we use are from the 19th century, and these are the same charts as used in your chartplotter. The above shows our track according to the chartplotter when in fact we were entering the harbour at Kastellorizon nearly quarter of a mile west.

charts they use on plotters or running under software on a laptop computer are somehow more advanced and up-to-date than paper charts. In fact they are exactly the same charts either scanned or digitised for use in the hardware. Often you will find on electronic charts that the boat icon is running across a cape or a headland and at anchor you are parked on the land. This discrepancy exists precisely because the GPS position is accurate, but there is no chart accurate enough to plot the position on.

All hydrographic and cartographic institutions are working to patch up the old charts as best they can. At Imrays I will frequently be asked why my GPS position for such and such a harbour does not agree exactly with the chart position corrected to WGS84. The answer is simply that I was there and

that my waypoint is the WGS84 position in the real world as opposed to the chart. At one time in the Med, errors of up to a mile were, if not common, frequent enough to be worrying. Over the years they have lessened but there are still errors of a quarter of a mile in some places and there may be larger ones elsewhere. What this all boils down to in the end is that you must not blindly rely on the charts you use. While you may know your position to ±5 metres, the chart you are navigating with may have an accuracy of ± a quarter of a mile.

What this means to craft navigating in any waters is that some circle of error (COE) around the boat must be used when close to dangers to navigation. Just what COE you use is difficult to sort out. In the Red Sea I used a minimum COE of one mile, but extended it to 1½ miles off places like Eritrea and Yemen when it seemed that there were large discrepancies. In the eastern Mediterranean you can probably get by with a COE of less than half a mile and in Spain, France and Italy a COE of quarter of a mile. Strangely enough, the most accurate charts I know of (GPS-wise) are around Cuba, as the Russians resurveyed all Cuban waters in the 1950s and 60s. I guess the moral in all this is not to be blinded by new electronic nav systems. Remember that the advice on start-up, that 'this instrument is an aid to navigation', must always be heeded. Don't forget all those old-fashioned coastal navigation techniques utilising a hand-bearing compass and eyeball navigation coupled to aids like radar and a depth-sounder which are so essential when navigating close to land and dangers to navigation.

Plotters and laptops

Plotters

A lot of yachts use a dedicated chart plotter interfaced to the GPS and in some cases to radar and instruments. It is a useful tool for navigation and I use one on *Skylax*. When choosing a chart plotter, bear the following in mind:

- Some screens are more easily read than others. Obviously, a good colour display will be more effective than greyscale, but with either, make sure that the plotter is positioned so that light on the screen does not make it difficult to read or identify aids and dangers to navigation.

The bigger the screen the better, but this depends on your budget. Get a protective cover on the new breed of screens as they scratch very easily and soon become difficult to read.

- Some plotters have an easier and more intuitive keypad and menu system than others. Think about what it will be like operating the keypad and cursor when it gets a bit bumpy at sea.

- Check on the price of chart cartridges and coverage. You may be surprised to find out how much it costs to get electronic chart cartridges for plotters and as a rule of thumb, they will cost more than equivalent charts for software running on a laptop.

- All plotters will have a small backup battery (usually lithium) to save your settings and data. These usually have to be replaced every three years or so. Carry a spare and enquire about how easy it is to replace the backup battery – they are often soldered onto a couple of wires and tucked away inside.

- Always plan longer passages on a paper chart. Chart plotters and charts on a laptop computer will not show rocks, reefs and even small islands until you get down to around 1:150,000 or even 1:100,000. Electronic charts can be raster or vector. Raster charts are a scanned copy of the paper chart, vector charts are digital databases. Raster charts are used by Maptech, SoftChart, British Admiralty (ARCS) and Imray amongst others. Vector charts are used by C-Map, Navionics, and Garmin. Depending on the resolution of the screen vector charts and some raster charts will not show all the detail when zoomed out. This can be dangerous if you are plotting a course over longer distances when it will appear that there are no dangers en route. Only by zooming in and panning along the whole route will you come across dangers to navigation. Plot passages on a paper chart where even on a small scale chart there will at least be a dot or cross and usually the name alongside it. There have been a number of yachts lost because passages have been planned on electronic charts without picking up on dangers along the route.

Laptop computers

A lot of yachts now have laptop computers on board and as well as being used for boat business and e-mails, they can also run software packages that reproduce charts and interface to the GPS and radar. One of the problems with most systems is that the laptop is not fitted into the navigation area and so is difficult to use when conditions are rough. Most people don't want to risk their laptop slithering all over the place when things get a bit lumpy. If you are contemplating a laptop-based navigation system, incorporating charts and instrumentation, then some thought needs to go into securing the laptop on the navigation table or perhaps as a modular unit with the screen on a bulkhead and the keyboard secured on the chart table. On *Skylax* I use industrial-strength Velcro to attach the laptop to the chart table; this holds it securely in place on passage – in fact it takes a bit of strength to 'rip' it off the chart table if you need to use it elsewhere.

You also need to remember that in a harsh marine environment, most laptops will be exposed to salt, humidity, temperature extremes and the boat's motion, conditions which they are not designed to operate in. Add to that the 'blue screen of death' when an error message or conflict comes up and you need to treat this option with caution.

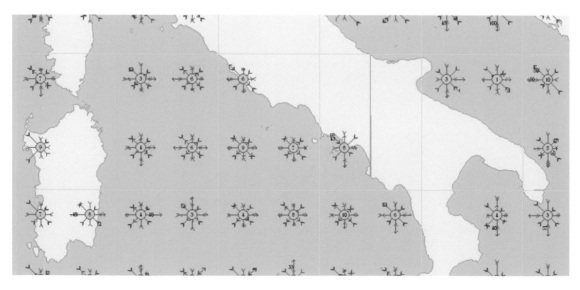

With a laptop on board, you can run routeing programmes and (as here) navigation software, download GRIB files and send e-mail, keep a log and even watch a DVD.

Nor does buying a titanium-clad monster make much sense when processing power increases almost weekly, making your expensive machine redundant after a year.

The following points should be kept in mind when looking at plotting software.

- You will need to choose between raster and vector charts. Basically raster charts are scanned originals. Vector charts are redrawn digitally from the original. In practice, the best choice is vector charts. They occupy less space on the hard disk, load more quickly and, importantly, can be read when you zoom in or out. Raster charts are scanned at one resolution so when you zoom in or out you lose definition and get a fuzzy, pixellated image. This is intensely irritating and the only answer is to buy a large folio of charts, although that means the laptop will be working hard loading charts on a smaller or larger scale. Raster charts also take longer to reload, which is annoying when you are trying to get from one side of the chart to the other on a laptop screen.
- Most charts come on a CD or memory stick of one kind or another, which you download on to the hard disk. Check what charts the software will support. Some software will only run the proprietary charts of the manufacturer, so you are stuck with their electronic charts. Some software will support a number of formats, although some formats like Maptech are more common than others such as the Admiralty ARCS charts. There is a move towards a universal format such as the open architecture NOS/ GEO/S57, but it is not yet widespread.
- Some chart-plotting software can overlay weather GRIB files on the chart. You can get up to a seven-day forecast on the internet. GRIB files can be downloaded from the internet or e-mailed if you have a pactor modem for the SSB, or a GSM or satellite phone like Iridium.
- Most modern computers have a USB port; to connect to an older GPS, which only has a serial plug (at present), you need a USB to serial converter cable. This will come with a driver for the USB-serial conversion which runs under Windows XP as well as Windows 98, ME, 2000 and iMac. Fire up the computer first and start the navigation programme before turning on the GPS or connecting the cable.
- Don't go for a chart plotter that has all the bells and whistles. Even a basic plotter has more than enough features for practical navigation and the more you squeeze onto a toolbar, the more confusing it gets when conditions get rough at sea. Even a basic plotter will insert waypoints, construct routes, let you keep an automatic log off the GPS input and an annotated log as well. Just as most of us never use half the functions on a word processor, so you will never need to use a lot of the functions on some chart plotters.
- Ease of use and large icons are important when it's blowing half a gale and the boat is bucketing to windward. You don't want to have to work out how to construct a route when the rest of the crew are sick and you are not feeling too bright yourself. And get a mouse for your laptop instead of using

the touchpad otherwise every time the boat hits a wave, the mouse pointer will shoot across the screen as you twiddle with it.

Warning

Although officially you can use something like the ARCS charts to replace paper charts, in practice you should think long and hard about both the legality and practicality of it. There have been prosecutions of small craft for not carrying paper charts when the chart plotter has broken down. In my own case I have had to revert to paper charts, which I carry anyway, when the hard disk on the laptop crashed. It can get even more silly. On the software I use, the authorisation code is written onto the hard disk. That worked fine until I defragged the hard disk. After that I could not load the software and was requested to e-mail the manufacturers

for a new authorisation code. This was impossible to do from Haiti where I was at the time.

Despite the usefulness of electronic charts, it does not totally replace the chart in the cockpit for me. I can put that old-fashioned paper chart anywhere, hold it up while looking at a feature or danger to navigation and quickly pan from one side of the chart to the other. You can get irritated with the 'please wait, chart loading' message on chart plotters as you either zoom in or out, or pan from one part to another. If the chart plotter is located at the chart table then you must constantly run up and down to check the map against the view above and this can make it difficult to mentally fit the 3D real view to the 2D chart view. A chart in the cockpit lets you constantly scan from one to the other and fit the chart to the real world.

POLARISED SUNGLASSES

Polarised plastic is known as a dichromic material and it transmits light only in one plane, typically the vertical. By cutting out the horizontal plane, polarised sunglasses effectively remove one plane of the reflected light on the surface of the sea; this allows us to see transmitted light bouncing off shallow areas such as reefs and sandy bottoms. These are the light blue, green and turquoise colours that identify underwater obstacles.

The value of polarised lenses in detecting just where a reef is and where the sandy patch is to drop anchor should not be under-estimated and normal sunglasses are not good enough. Here are some general rules for wearers of polarised sunglasses.

- Deep blue: 15m plus
- Turquoise: 10m
- Green: 5m
- Brown: you can identify marine species

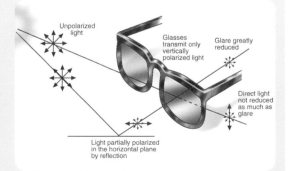

The view without polarised glasses...   ... and the view with.

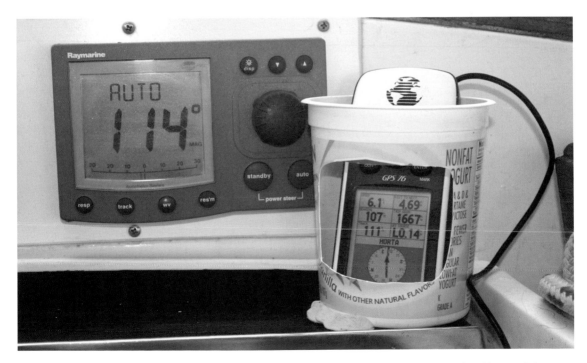

Get a backup GPS. Our new chart plotter with integrated GPS failed when just a few months old so until it was replaced we made do with the portable. Its special yoghurt-pot holder was because the internal aerial doesn't work down below.

One of the advantages of sailing in the Mediterranean is that the clarity of the water lets you check depths with your own 'wetware' between your ears, just by looking at the colour of the water. This is Cati in Turkey.

Real world navigation

There are some things that can be overlooked navigation-wise as perhaps peripheral or not worthy of weighty consideration, compared to which model of chart plotter or radar you are going to buy. In the real world of pilotage, when you are edging into a reef-fringed anchorage or taking a shallow shortcut passage, good vision is vitally important.

Mast-steps
Mast-steps or ratlines are a pretty common feature on yachts cruising around coral in tropical waters. They let you get high enough to clearly see coral reefs and coral heads. The Mediterranean has no coral reefs as such, but mast-steps will allow you to see underwater rocks and reefs a lot more easily, even if you only go up a couple of steps. For this reason, it is worth fitting them – at least up to the first set of crosstrees so you can climb up a little way to get a clearer view of what's going on. Apart from rocks and reefs, you can spot that elusive patch of sand for anchoring and mast-steps give you an easy start for going up the mast to check and repair rigging and masthead fittings. You will be surprised how much use you get out of them.

Charts and pilots
I write some of them so it's no surprise that I'm going to say that you will need

them. In the early days I managed with a minimum of small-scale charts and filled in the gaps with the pilot books I had. Nowadays I buy more large-scale charts for areas I'm going to cruise.

It's a good idea to buy your charts before you leave as some charts may be difficult to find in the Med itself and you will find yourself paying more money out there for an Admiralty or Imray chart. In Spain, France and Italy you can get hold of Spanish/French/Italian hydrographic department charts, although you will pay around the same amount of money or more than you would in the UK for an Admiralty chart. In Croatia and Greece you can buy local hydrographic charts although these will be in Cyrillic and Greek respectively. In Turkey you can buy Turkish hydrographic department charts at a competitive price.

Sometimes you just know where you are. The distinctive Rock of Gibraltar disappears astern.

Pilots are available for most of the Med countries although some areas get more skimpy coverage than others. Some people photocopy pilots and I have to say that this is a NO-NO. In practice there is little that can be done about copying (although see the section on the new SOLAS regulations on page 86), but it is both illegal and immoral to steal from publishers and authors.

In the chapter on Mediterranean countries and passage planning I give a comprehensive list of pilots and you can make your choice from these. It's worth bearing in mind that charts and pilots can be obtained second-hand from time to time so you can pick up your charts and pilots at much less than the new retail price. As long as these potentially out-of-date charts and pilots are used with care, you can get around safely with them and you may find them annotated with useful notes. Again, look at the new SOLAS regulations concerning this.

It is useful to have some charts and pilots well before you start passage planning so you can enjoy the wonderful anticipation of all the places you intend to visit. In addition, a few guide books covering your chosen countries will be useful for extra-curricular activities. The *Rough Guides* stand up pretty well and the *Lonely Planet* series is also useful. For more in-depth cultural and historical information try the *Blue Guides*, published by Somerset Books. There are also a lot of other one-off guides and some that are out of print such as the old Collins' *Companion Guides* (now being republished independently).

Ship's log

In the age of electronic charts and GPS, the humble ship's log is often neglected. You should keep one, and a log may be required to comply with SOLAS V regs. Apart from this, a log is necessary if your electronic/GPS fails and you need to start using dead reckoning to get to your destination. Below I have given a sample of the log headings I use, which can be printed off on a computer,

photocopied and given plastic spiral binding and laminated covers in a print shop. It may seem to contain a lot of useless data, but it all helps if you need to use dead reckoning and also provides a useful aide memoire. It may bring back a bit of the terror of the confused swell off the Seven Capes or the 45-knot *levanter* that stopped you getting into the Strait of Gibraltar.

Suggested ship's log format

NAME (of vessel):			REG NO:		OWNER:			GRT:			
Date	Time	Lat	Long	Wind	Sea	Barom (mb)	Course reqd	COG	Dist (NM)	Speed (knots)	SOG

COG – course over ground (or track) SOG – speed over ground

REMARKS (put on opposite page)

SOLAS REGS

From 1 July 2002, skippers of craft under 150 tons were required to conform to the following SOLAS V regulations. The regs will probably only be applied piecemeal in Med countries, if at all in some. Nonetheless you should be aware of them. What follows is very much my précis of the regs and, at the time of writing, clarification was still ongoing.

- R19 A radar reflector (3 & 9 GHz) must be exhibited.
- R29 A table of life-saving signals must be available to the skipper/helmsman at all times. The RYA produces a suitable table.
- R31 Skippers must report to the Coastguard on dangers to navigation including (R32)

wrecks, winds of force 10 or more and floating objects dangerous to navigation.
- R33 Vessels must respond to distress signals from another vessel.
- R34 Safe Navigation and Avoidance of Dangerous Situations. Vessels must be able to demonstrate that adequate passage planning has been undertaken. Things like weather, tides, vessel limitations, crew, navigational dangers and contingency plans should be addressed.
- R35 Distress signals must not be misused.
- Contact the RYA (www.rya.org.uk) for more information on how SOLAS V relates to pleasure craft.

7 Weather

Weather in the Mediterranean can come as a bit of a shock for those unfamiliar with the place. The image of the Med as a deep blue lake ruffled by the occasional zephyr blowing out of an azure sky is not the whole picture.

On average, there is more wind around the Mediterranean than around northern European shores. For example, at four locations along the south coast of England, average wind speeds over the year are 8, 9, 9, 9 knots. At four locations along the south coast of France the annual average wind speeds are 11, 11, 9, 8 knots. It certainly can blow in the Med and sometimes it can blow too much. The *meltemi* screaming down through the Aegean for days can set teeth on edge and you wonder when it will end. At the western end, the *levanter* hurtles through the Straits of Gibraltar, making it difficult for small ships trying to enter the Med and causing eddies over the Rock that can complicate landings at Gibraltar airport.

But if there are strong winds in the Mediterranean (and calms too), for the most part they are predictable. The beginning and end of the *meltemi* in the Aegean, its strength and direction, has been plotted since antiquity. *Meltemi* (from the Turkish meaning bad-tempered) and the ancients' *etesians* (from the Greek *etios* meaning annual), were used by merchant ships to sail south, where they waited until the autumn southerlies to come north again. At certain times of the year, many of the big merchant fleets of the Middle Ages were prohibited to leave harbour until the bad winter weather had gone. In the western Mediterranean the sea breeze reigns supreme and apart from the odd rogue *mistral* or *tramontana*, you can safely get about on sea breezes for most of the summer.

The idea that the Mediterranean summer is one of light zephyrs on a calm sea is a confusion concerning the predictable patterns of the season. A settled summer where thermal winds predominate does not mean a summer without fresh to strong winds. The blue sea can be quickly covered with whitecaps and steep waves whipped up by a wind blowing out of a clear azure sky. It's easy to confuse predictability and settled conditions with calm weather and light zephyrs and most us have a picture postcard view of oily calm Med days. Even I can forget this until I return. After a voyage to Southeast Asia and back, and after beating up the Red Sea in winds constantly in the 25–35 knot range, I emerged from Port Said en route to Turkey and, for the first time in the entire trip, had to heave-to for 8 hours in 45 knot winds. Likewise on returning from the Caribbean and getting through

In general, you will get more wind in the Mediterranean than around UK waters. The wet-weather gear is for keeping dry – not warm.

the Strait of Gibraltar without a *levanter*, I had to hole up in the Balearics for a week while 40–50 knot winds battered the islands. It's just as well that our 'wetware' has such poor long-term memory for bad weather.

There is a common mantra in the Med, often repeated in bars and harbours, that there is either 'too much wind or too little wind'. There is some truth in it but more often than not it is used as an excuse for poor planning. Weather in the Med is indeed tricky to predict and often needs careful handling. That said, any well-found yacht will not have any problems dealing with the weather as long as proper passage planning and proper seamanship skills are employed. Too often yachts on passage have decided they are going to x harbour or anchorage and have not researched alternative ports of refuge should the weather change dramatically. It's almost as if, having

once decided that x is the spot, then come what may you have to go there. In the Med this is just plain silly when there are usually so many alternatives scattered around the coast and islands.

One thing that often catches people out is the speed with which the weather can change. In the UK you watch the depressions plodding across the Atlantic and, depending on their track and speed, can make a good educated guess about what is going to happen. In the Med strong winds can blow suddenly out of a clear sky and within half an hour the sea will change from an oily calm to a wave-tossed force 7. Thermal winds in the summer are not the gentle sea breezes that blow onto the English coast but are stronger beasts often blowing at force 5–6. Depressions in the Mediterranean, although often small by Atlantic standards, can be fierce affairs that deepen quickly, stop and start erratically, and keep you guessing about the track they are going to take.

Summer

The climate of the Mediterranean can be divided into settled sunny summers and violent wet winters. The difference between the two is difficult to describe until you see it for yourself. Often I'm asked why I don't spend all my winters in the Mediterranean. Apart from the fact I have to work, it is just a lot colder and wetter than most people seem to think.

The specific climate of the Med is produced by the high mountain ranges in the north, which cut it off from the Continental climate of Europe and also from much of the Atlantic influence. In the south, the Sahara is a thermal heat sink that also influences the Mediterranean climate, pushing warm air north onto the sea.

In Britain and northern France, the changeable Atlantic climate predominates, bringing variable summer weather. In eastern Europe and Russia the extremes of the Continental climate dictate the weather. The Mediterranean climate is separated, to a degree, from the Atlantic and Continental systems by the mountains fringing its northern edge: those of the Iberian Peninsula, and of the French, Swiss and Austrian Alps, and the Balkans. In the summer the Med locks into its own cyclonic system that produces the predictable summers. From early June until late September, a high pressure system sits over the central southern Mediterranean, affecting the weather from the Straits of Gibraltar to the Aegean. This stable weather pattern, along with the Azores high, halts the ingress of depressions into the Mediterranean, with the result that all weather is local weather.

Most of this local weather is thermally induced with sea breezes providing the important strong winds up to force 6. By funnelling and deflection along a shore they can occasionally reach gale force. Most of the land around the Med is high steep-to land and the wind will often scream down the lee side of capes and islands with a ferocity that surprises sailors from northern climes.

Depending on which direction the coast is facing, the sea breeze may set in earlier or later depending on when the sun starts to warm up the land. A south-facing coast will get sun earlier and for longer than a north-facing coast, so we can expect the sea breeze to start earlier and blow harder on a south-facing coast than on a north-facing coast. The general mechanics for a sea breeze, depending on the direction the coast faces, are shown on page 91. These mechanics are obviously influenced by all sorts of other variables including other pressure systems around, other nearby landmasses, and the height of the land.

The wind clock concept depends on the orientation of the coastline and the time of year, but the theory usually holds good for most of the Mediterranean summer. There are some important exceptions, which are discussed later, and it is important to understand that other pressure differences may affect the sea breeze, but certain conditions can be predicted. Thus nights are usually calm, giving you a good night's sleep at anchor. In the early morning there may be a light breeze blowing off the land at perhaps 10 knots, but usually less. Around midday or early afternoon the sea breeze will fill in and blow until dusk or just after. It is real gentlemen's sailing with calm nights and a brisk afternoon breeze for a short passage along the coast. Should the prevailing wind be in the wrong direction, then you can choose to get up early and motor to your next port of call, or thrash to windward in the afternoon, depending on your inclination.

The sea breeze theory sounds delightfully simple, but coastline configuration can cause exceptions. Lee eddies caused by a gulf or a large bay can reverse winds. The wind 20 miles off a coast can be radically different from that

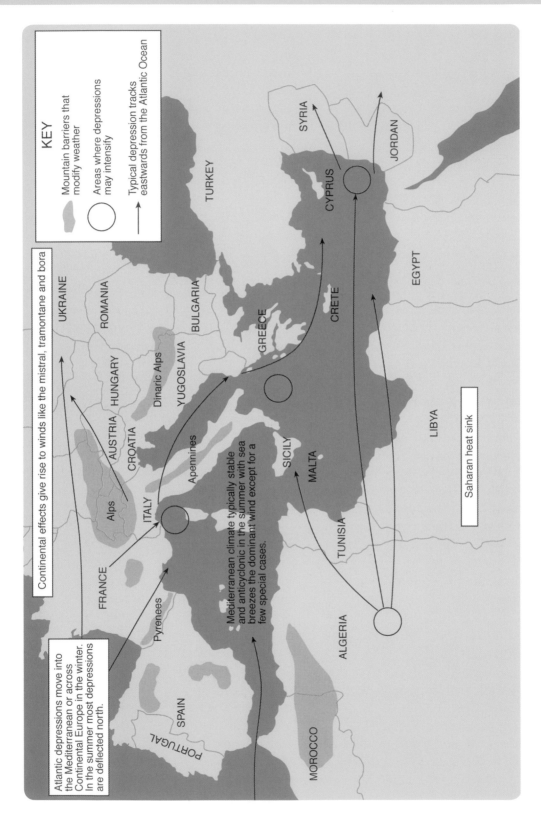

Continental effects give rise to winds like the mistral, tramontane and bora

KEY

Mountain barriers that modify weather

Areas where depressions may intensify

Typical depression tracks eastwards from the Atlantic Ocean

Atlantic depressions move into the Mediterranean or across Continental Europe in the winter. In the summer most depressions are deflected north.

Mediterranean climate typically stable and anticyclonic in the summer with sea breezes the dominant wind except for a few special cases.

Saharan heat sink

UKRAINE
ROMANIA
BULGARIA
TURKEY
GREECE
CRETE
SYRIA
CYPRUS
JORDAN
EGYPT
LIBYA
HUNGARY
AUSTRIA
CROATIA
YUGOSLAVIA
Dinaric Alps
Apennines
Alps
ITALY
FRANCE
Pyrenees
SICILY
MALTA
TUNISIA
ALGERIA
MOROCCO
SPAIN
PORTUGAL

A map of the Mediterranean Sea showing climate types and effects, depression tracks and mountain barriers.

SEA BREEZES

The mechanics of the sea breeze are the same as around any coast. When the land warms to a temperature above that of the water it creates a pressure difference that draws a breeze in from the sea. The general wind clock operates for most Med countries and works like this:

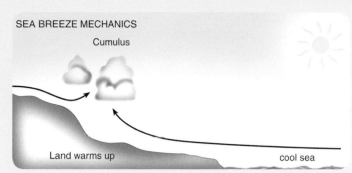

SEA BREEZE MECHANICS

Cumulus

Land warms up   cool sea

0800 – 1200 Land warms up and cumuli start to form. Initially there will usually be a calm with a light onshore wind as the sea breeze begins to build.
1200 – 1500 A sea breeze begins to build and large cumuli form over land.
1500 – 1800 The sea breeze is at its strongest; it can build to force 6 and there may be gusts off high slopes.

1800 – 2000 The sea breeze dies, often abruptly towards the end.
2000 – 0800 Often it may be calm or there may be a light offshore land breeze, usually around 2200 onwards. The land breeze rarely gets above force 4. In the spring and autumn in mountainous areas there may be a katabatic wind which can get up to force 7–8 for a few hours.

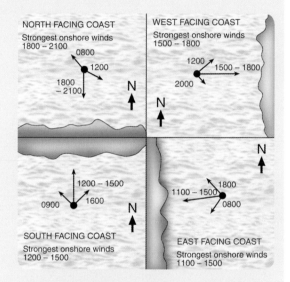

NORTH FACING COAST
Strongest onshore winds
1800 – 2100
0800
1200
1800 – 2100

WEST FACING COAST
Strongest onshore winds
1500 – 1800
1200
1500 – 1800
2000

SOUTH FACING COAST
Strongest onshore winds
1200 – 1500
1200 – 1500
0900   1600

EAST FACING COAST
Strongest onshore winds
1100 – 1500
1800
1100 – 1500
0800

The sea breeze clock concept is an effective way of working out the wind direction and strength along much of the Mediterranean coastline. The 'hands' of the clock show wind direction.

inshore. Special winds like the *mistral* or *bora* can violently override the prevailing sea breeze. Also, in the Aegean, a pressure difference between an established area of high pressure in the Balkans and relatively low pressure over the Cyprus region pulls the *meltemi* in a large arc from the Black Sea through the Aegean to Crete and Rhodes. These coastal effects all need to be taken into account as most of the sailing in the Mediterranean is at 20 miles, or less, off the coast.

Coastal effects

Many of the coastal effects described here will be familiar to most yachtsmen. Moving air takes the path of least resistance so where there is high land near the coast, it is deflected, funnelled and channelled according to the shape of the land. What most people will not be familiar with is the extent to which the land modifies the wind in the Mediterranean. Around the relatively flat coastline of northern Europe, coastal effects are often negligible. In the Mediterranean the land is often steep-to with high mountain ranges climbing sharply out of the water. This particular topography means that there is ten times the coastal effect that you would get in northern Europe; for example, whilst a 20 knot breeze over flat water might be compressed to 23 or 25 knots in northern Europe, in the Med you often find a 20 knot breeze gusting off high land at 30 knots or more. Treat the effects with caution.

- Wind blowing onto, or at an angle to, the coast will freshen close to the land. The land offers more resistance than the sea and where there are high cliffs or mountains the wind is simply blocked from blowing over the land.
- Around a high headland or cape, the wind will follow the contours of the land. The compression of the wind against the land increases its strength so inevitably you get gusts from different directions in these areas. The gusts push the sea from different directions and cause a confused sea around headlands so it will often pay

to stand some distance off.

- When the wind increases above a certain strength it may start to gust over the headland or cape, depending on the topography. On the wind-ward side there will be light winds of variable direction where the wind has lifted, while on the leeward side there will be strong gusts, often 10 or 20 knots higher than the prevailing wind over the open sea. This always seems to catch out newcomers from northern Europe and it is important you take this into consideration as these winds, compressed and funnelled to take the easiest path over the lowest bit of land or down a valley, can lead to quite ferocious squalls on the lee side of capes and islands.
- Where the wind blows into a channel or gap, say between islands, it will tend to follow the channel rather than blow across the land, and so it is channelled and speeded up. It can also bend round and, for example, a useful beam wind outside can become a headwind in a restricted channel, or variable. You may then have to short-tack or motor to get through.
- Where a wind is establishing itself against an opposing wind there will be a buffer zone of variables in between, which can be several miles or as little as 100 metres across. In a narrow buffer zone, the incongruous sight of a boat running one way approaching another running in the opposite direction can take a minute to comprehend.

It is all very well talking about these effects, but it is perhaps more instructive to see just how they can modify the

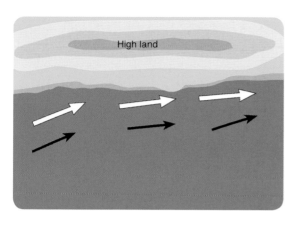

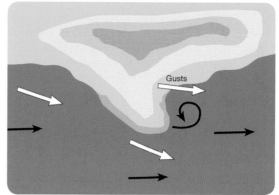

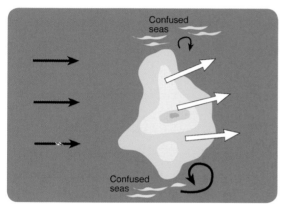

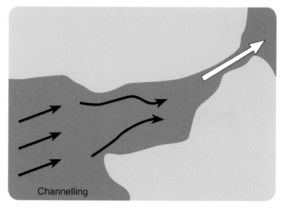

prevailing breeze. In the Ionian in Greece, the sea breeze, the *maistros*, gets up around midday and blows consistently at 10–25 knots from the north-west. In the inland sea where I spent a lot of years chartering, this wind can be deflected and funnelled and channelled so it blows from the north, the west and even south-west to south in places. The diagram here shows how the prevailing wind is modi-fied around Levkas.

Other winds

In the summer, and also in the autumn and spring, there are a number of other winds that do not strictly fit the thermal

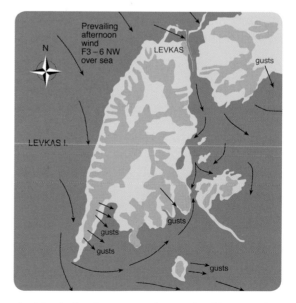

The island of Levkas is a good example of how wind can be channelled in many directions.

93

wind pattern although they can be modified, or directly caused by thermal effects other than the sea breeze patterns.

Meltemi

The *meltemi* is a special case. It blows in the Aegean in the summer and is the prevailing wind. From June until September the *meltemi* blows from the Black Sea down through the Aegean to Crete and Rhodes and the adjacent Turkish coast as far as Finike. In July and August it is often force 6–7 with stronger gusts off high land. As already mentioned, the *meltemi* is a result of a pressure gradient between the Balkan high and an area of relatively low pressure over Cyprus. The coastal effects previously described cause it to curve round to blow from the west into the gulfs along the Turkish coast, and it is funnelled and channelled over and around the islands of the Aegean. It has a thermal component, in that it will often die down in the early morning and, like the sea breeze, is at its strongest in the late afternoon.

Katabatic winds

At night, when the tops of the mountains and hills cool before the land and sea at the bottom, cold air flows down the slopes. On the way it gathers momentum as more air cools and adds to the wind. Where it is funnelled by a valley it can reach force 6–7 at sea level. Katabatic winds arrive without warning, often blowing in from the opposite direction of the prevailing daytime wind. They are most likely in spring and autumn but where they are known to be frequent, it pays to take special care. In most cases they are over in a couple of hours, but off mountains such as the high Taurus in eastern Turkey they have been known to blow at force 7–8 for most of the night.

Anabatic winds

The wind flows uphill when mountain slopes are warmer than the valleys: this occurs in the early morning when the upper slopes get sun and the lower slopes and valleys are shaded. As it rarely exceeds 5 knots it does not pose the same threat as the katabatic wind.

Thunderstorms

In unstable air when cumulus and cumulo-nimbus clouds form thunderstorms, there can be a severe squall produced by the rush of rain falling down through the

CORIOLIS EFFECT

In North Europe sea breezes are not usually strong enough to be affected by this, but in the Mediterranean they are. The Coriolis effect results from the Earth spinning on its axis and deflecting objects from a straight path; it has to be taken into account when a shell is fired from a field gun, for example. In the northern hemisphere, the deflection is towards the right so that winds are deflected slightly to the west. This westerly deflection can be detected in most of the prevailing winds of the Mediterranean and even a 'pure' onshore sea breeze will have a westerly deflection to it, giving winds an easterly component, all other things (topography and other pressure systems) being equal.

cloud. There will be little warning of this wind apart from the visible cloud, falling rain, thunder and lightning. You can gauge your distance from a thunderstorm by dividing by five the number of seconds between seeing the lightning and hearing the thunder, which gives the distance in miles. Typically, the downdraft produced by the rain arrives in seconds with the peak gusts at the very beginning of the squall. As these gusts commonly reach force 6–7, a thunderstorm is not something to be trifled with. If you appear to be on a collision course with one it is prudent to take precautions and get the sails off, or at least reef drastically. The squall from a thunderstorm may last only minutes or several hours.

In the summer the meltemi blows strongly down through the Aegean. This is Manganari on Ios with 40+ knot gusts into the bay.

Winter

Winter in the Mediterranean comes as a malevolent mocking of the settled sunny summer. It rains; it hails; it snows. Depressions roar in from the Atlantic bringing storms that break down harbour walls and rip the tiles off roofs. The violence of a Mediterranean winter is wholly unexpected by those who have not experienced one before. In spring, the winter weather rapidly recedes, earlier in the east than farther west and north. In the autumn, winter weather arrives quickly and violently with torrential rain and thunderstorms, although there is usually a brief respite in November, a sort of Mediterranean 'Indian summer' (to jumble up two disparate parts of the world).

Although it is possible to sail in the winter, most yachts are laid up by November. The south-eastern part of the Mediterranean is the most popular for those determined to potter about in the winter, but even here passages need to be planned with a port of refuge within easy reach. In the western Mediterranean, few yachts venture out in the winter except for day-sailing.

In the spring and autumn, the sailing can be superb although keep an eye on the weather, especially in March and October. At the end of the summer the air temperatures drop from the stifling highs of July and August, and in spring the land is covered with a profusion of wild flowers and a vivid green unimaginable a few months later.

While the summer is basically a period of thermal winds, in the winter the Atlantic effect seeps into the Med and sends depressions either directly into it

95

or to the north across Europe or south across North Africa. These low pressure systems affect the weather in the Med and the predictable summer patterns no longer apply. In the spring and autumn, low pressure systems will also affect the weather and even in summer normal patterns can be influenced by low pressure systems sneaking in – usually it is the west that suffers while eastern Mediterranean weather patterns remain fairly stable.

On the north side of the Med, lows enter through the Rhône Valley or through the Alps into the Gulf of Genoa. In the Gulf of Genoa a depression will frequently deepen and then move eastwards, bringing gale-force winds and torrential rain to the eastern Mediterranean. The Genoa lee cyclone gives rise to some of the strongest

winds and frequently halts shipping in its vicinity. Depressions also come through the Straits of Gibraltar and move eastwards or occasionally sweep across the top of North Africa.

The highest winter gale frequency occurs in the Gulf of Lions with an average of 12 gales in the winter. In the Balearics the average is four and in the sea area between Sardinia and Sicily it is also four. In the Ionian the average is four while in the Aegean it increases to eight. Although these figures give us an idea of gale frequencies, they do not necessarily represent the frequency of gale-force winds. Small disturbances that hardly nudge the barometer can cause violent winds with little or no warning. Large thunderstorms can generate 50–60 knot gusts. And a strong breeze can be

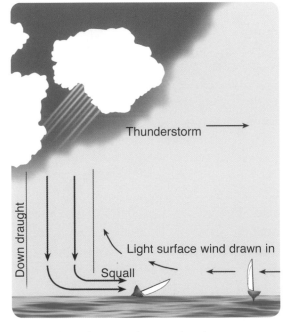

The typical wind pattern during a thunderstorm.

Out of season, keep an eye on the weather and learn to recognise cloud formations.

funnelled through a gap causing gale-force winds. As in the summer, the local topography plays havoc with wind direction and velocity.

To some extent, the winter weather patterns are more like typical weather patterns further north and assessing them is a matter of tracking depressions coming into or near the Mediterranean. The problem here is that the sea and high land mean that depressions do not plod steadily across the Med and occasionally loiter here or there as they encounter other pressure obstacles. Their progress is often erratic and it is difficult to know what track they will take. Often they will deepen and at times may just peter out. Fortunately, weather forecasts have much improved in the Med in the last decade, and the sort of weather information now

LOCAL NAMES FOR MEDITERRANEAN WINDS

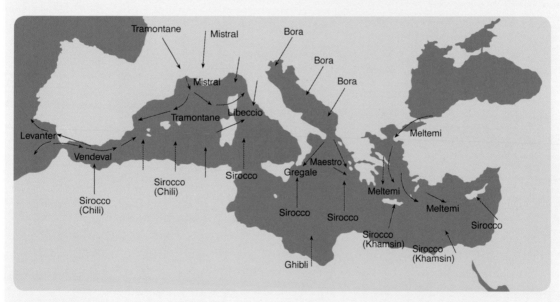

A map of the Mediterranean showing the local names for winds.

These names do not indicate frequency, but often they are specially named because they disturb the normal wind patterns or are exceptionally violent.

Arifi Strong sirocco in Morocco.

Bise Cold, dry north-easterly in the Languedoc-Rousillon region.

Bora Violent coastal-slope wind blowing off the Balkans (and the Karst and Dinaric Alps) into the Adriatic.

Borasco Gale with squalls and thunderstorms in Italy; predominantly westerly and south-westerly.

Borini Small *bora* on the Italian Adriatic coast.

Bura Another name for *bora*.

Chergui Warm dry *sirocco* in Morocco.

Chili Hot, dry *sirocco* in Tunisia and Algeria.

Chom Hot, dry southerly in Algeria.

Dzhani Warm, dry southerly in North Africa.

Etesians Ancient name for the *meltemi*, no longer commonly used.

Gharbi Strong, moist, dust-laden south-westerly in Morocco; brings the 'red rain' to France, Italy and Greece. Known as the *gharbis* in Italy and Greece.

Ghibli Strong *sirocco* in Tunisia.

Gregale Strong north-easterly blowing over the Tyrrhenian and Ionian seas to Malta; associated with a *bora*. Also called *grecale* – the 'Greek wind'.

Imbat Sea breeze in North Africa, also the local name for the *meltemi* in the Gulf of Izmir.

Khamsin Hot, dry *sirocco* in Egypt.

Levante Strong east to north-easterly wind blowing onto the Spanish coast. It builds up a big swell across the comparatively long fetch.

Levanter Easterly winds blowing through the Straits of Gibraltar.

Levenche Hot, dry, dust-laden south-easterly blowing onto southern Spain.

Llevantades Gales from the north-east in eastern Spain.

Libeccio West or south-westerlies in Italy. Can be strong and accompanied by squalls and thunderstorms.

Maestral Northerlies in France.

Maestrale Cold, dry *mistral* type wind in the Gulf of Genoa.

Maestro Sea breeze in the Adriatic and the Greek Ionian. Also called *maistro*.

Marin Warm humid, dust-laden southerlies in the Gulf of Lions; similar to the *leveche*.

Meltemi Strong northerlies becoming westerly in the Aegean. Also *meltem* in Turkey and the *etesians* to the ancient Greeks.

Mestrale Northerlies in Spain similar to the *maestral*.

Mistral Cold, dry, strong winds blowing out of the Rhône Valley into the Gulf of Lions, often as far as the Balearics and Sardinia.

Ponente Westerlies in Italy and Greece.

Sharav Hot, dry *sirocco* in Israel.

Simoom Hot, dry, desert wind in North Africa. Literally means 'the poisoner'; also called *simoon*.

Sirocco Hot, dry, southerlies from North Africa. They pick up moisture over the sea to become humid and oppressive winds by the time they reach European shores.

Tramontana A *bora* which extends to Corsica and Sardinia.

Tramontane Cold dry wind blowing out of the Toulouse Gap into the Gulf of Lions and Spain similar to the *mistral*.

Vardarac A *bora* type wind in the Aegean, especially the Gulf of Thessaloniki.

Vendeval Westerly winds in the Straits of Gibraltar; also called *vendevales*.

available is light years ahead of what it once was. There are good internet weather sources and Navtex and VHF forecasts are now more widely available. Using what information you have, it is a matter of tracking depressions and trying to predict what will happen just as you do anywhere else. That said, there are some special cases:

Mistral and tramontane

I lump these two together because they are caused by the same process and in fact a *tramontane* is often mistakenly called a *mistral*. These are mountain-gap winds that blow when a low-pressure system crosses into France from the Atlantic and cold air piles up in central France. There are two escape routes for the cold air. A *tramontane* blows out of the Toulouse Gap between the Massif Central and the Pyrenees. It blows from the north-west and fans out to the east and west in the Gulf of Lions. It can extend past the Balearics and to Corsica. A *mistral* blows down the Rhône Valley and into the Gulf of Lions and likewise fans out towards the Balearics and Corsica. These winds can arrive without warning and go from a flat calm to 50 knots in an hour. The sky is typically electric blue with no distinctive cloud cover. It is a ferocious wind and contributes to much of the high gale frequency in the Gulf of Lions. Strabo, the Greek geographer, described it as 'an impetuous and terrible wind which displaces rocks, hurls men from their chariots, breaks their limbs and strips them of their clothes and weapons'.

Force 9 in the Aegean with an earlier victim of Aegean weather on the rocks.

Bora

Like the *mistral*, the *bora* occurs when a cold front moves across Italy into the Balkans and cold air pours out through the mountain gap at the top of the Adriatic. The *bora* blows from the north-east down into the Adriatic and like the *mistral* the wind can rise to 50 knots and more within an hour. Other similar mountain-gap winds are the *vardarac* that blows from the north into the Gulf of Thessaloniki and the *bora* (same name but different wind) that blows down into the Black Sea.

Sirocco

A desert wind that blows off the Sahara bringing hot air to Europe. It blows off the desert when a series of lows pass eastward across the Mediterranean. As

it crosses the sea, it picks up moisture, bringing a leaden sultriness to the European shores. It commonly blows up into the Tyrrhenian and Adriatic Sea. It is said that if the *sirocco* blows for more than three days in Sicily, all inexplicable crimes of passion are excused; certainly it produces an oppressive and unpleasant atmosphere, as well as depositing the red sand of the Sahara over everything. The *sirocco* is most common in the spring but occurs at other times as well. It can blow a gale, but its force is normally less than this. In different parts of the Med it is known by different names: *levante* in Spain, *leveche* in Morocco, *chergui* in Algeria, *chili* in Tunisia, *ghibli* in Libya, *khamsin* in Egypt, and *sharav* in Israel.

Levanter

The *levanter* is the scourge of all boats trying to get in through the Strait of

Gibraltar. It blows from the east and is funnelled out through the Strait. Commonly there can be 10 or 15 knots 20 miles east of Gibraltar while in the Strait there is half a gale blowing. The *levanter* is the prevailing wind in the summer and winter, and most gales are from this direction.

Weather forecasts

Weather forecasts can be obtained from a number of sources. I'll detail the sources here but for specifics you will need to refer to the relevant pilot or almanac.

VHF
Most countries transmit forecasts on VHF at specific times and in the case of Italy on a continuous loop forecast (Ch 68). Most of these forecasts will be preceded by a securité announcement on Ch 16 so if you are unsure, keep monitoring Ch 16. Many of the forecasts are in English and times and frequencies can be obtained from the relevant pilot.

In general VHF forecasts are more accurate for areas in the Mediterranean because they have been interpolated from various data sources by a meteorologist. Thus is not to say that meteorologists get it right all the time, but there is a better chance that they will compared to grib models.

GRIB files
GRIB files are computer generated and rely principally on models using pressure differences to predict wind speed and direction. Various forecasters use different grib models, but the only ones freely available are from NOAA and the US Navy. The NOAA model, GFS, is the model commonly used by free internet sites. The US Navy NOGAPS and WW3 models are not dissimilar and in any case WW3 is not useful for the Mediterranean. A GRIB file is a compressed binary file that can be delivered on an internet site or by an email request.

It's important to know that GRIB files do not have any input from a forecaster's grey matter that will assess the effects of land masses, frontal activity and squalls, and local geographical anomalies. They are not good at modelling thermal effects and the topographical effects of land masses and localised sea temperature differences.

In the Mediterranean it's not surprising that, with large land masses around that heat up and cool at different rates depending on their orientation to the sun, that there are significant thermal effects that GRIBs do not get right. Add to that the effects of channelling and funnelling from land

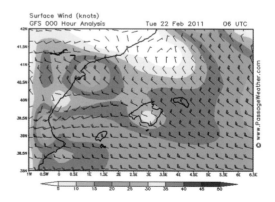

Passageweather GRIB files for the Balearics and adjacent Spanish coast.

masses and complex pressure differences over the land and sea that you don't always get over open water and the result is that you must not expect accurate forecasts from GRIB models.

Some forecasters use interpolations for various influences on pressure and wind, but even this fine tuning cannot deliver accurate forecasts all the time. That's not to say that GRIBs are not useful – they are. But they are not the be-all and end-all for forecasts and it's up to you to interpret the GRIBs and use them as one part of your forecast along with data from other sources.

SSB

There are a few SSB weather sources that can be found in the relevant pilot or almanac, but probably the best use of SSB is as part of a net when you can get data from someone in a particular area or with access to weather data from that area.

Mediterranean net:
0700 zulu 07085kHz Ham net.

Broadcast radio

In many countries there is a forecast on MF or FM although some of the forecasts are vague and not at all like the much loved BBC Shipping Forecast.

Telephone and text

In a number of countries you can phone or text for a forecast. A charge (often quite hefty) is invariably made for this service nowadays.

Navtex

All transmissions in the Mediterranean are on 518 kHz for English and 490 KHz for local language services, and there is good coverage for most of the Med. Very often Navtex text forecasts deliver the same information as VHF voice broadcasts. There have been reports of bad coverage or missed messages, but I have not encountered problems anywhere in the Mediterranean. The one thing you may get during unusual atmospheric conditions is a forecast for an area well outside your own Navtex range where the station has the same signifier as one you want to listen to. As it is unlikely the transmission times will be the same, this is not usually a problem, but it's worth being aware of. Navtex is useful because it automatically picks up forecasts and also Notices to Mariners. It provides very cost-effective weather information.

Weatherfax

A number of useful weatherfax transmissions can be picked up in the Mediterranean, but lately a number of stations have been discontinued and it is likely the service will grind down in the next few years as e-mail and internet services replace it.

Internet

There are numerous excellent sources for weather data on the internet and internet cafés can be found in most medium-sized towns.

If you have internet capability on board it is a weather source that is likely to eclipse many other 'steam' sources like Weatherfax and SSB. On page 102 I list a few sites, but remember that web addresses change frequently.

WEATHER ON THE INTERNET

General sites

- Weather Online:
  www.weatheronline.co.uk/sail.htm gives surface wind direction and strength up to a week ahead.
- JCOMM GMDSS by Meteo France:
  //weather.gmdss.com is the official text forecast for GMDSS MSI. Select METAREA III.
- DWD German Weather Forecasting:
  www.dwd.de Follow links to Wetter + klima; Wetter Aktuell; Seewetter; Mittelmeer. This is a German language site but contains easily understood tabled forecasts and detailed 3-day text forecasts for W Med areas.
- Frank Singleton's Weather Site:
  www.franksingleton.clara.net is an excellent overview of weather for sailors, with comprehensive links to weather sources.
- Mediterranean Sea Weather Page:
  www.stop.com/atol/ gives a BBC Synoptic map, Bracknell surface analysis map, surface analysis maps from USN Rota and wind charts from the University of Athens. Text forecasts from NOAA.
- Other general sites include:
  www.windfinder.com,
  www.meteosail.com and
  www.weatherweb.net (Atlantic)

Country-specific sites

- Spanish Meteorological Service:
  www.inm.es is a comprehensive site in Spanish only.
- Meteo France: www.meteofrance.com contains detailed forecasts for coastal and offshore areas in W Med.
- Italian National Meteorological Service:
  www.meteoam.it contains meteomar text of forecasts as on VHF Ch 68.
- Eurometeo: www.eurometeo.com gives up to

a three-day forecast with wind strength and sea conditions for all Italian waters.
- Italian aeronautical forecasts: www.meteoam.it
- Sardinian Regional Weather site:
  www.sar.sardegna.it gives local forecasts for Italian waters.
- Malta Airport: www.maltaairport.com gives three-day forecasts, text, graphics and synoptic charts.
- National Met Service:
  //meteo.hr/index_en.php for Croatia
- Poseidon weather for Greece:
  www.poseidon.ncmr.gr/weather_forecast.html gives up to 72-hour surface wind forecasts for Greece. The best source of weather for Greek and adjacent Turkish waters.
- Hellenic National Meteorological Service:
  www.hnms.gr contains text forecasts as given in radio broadcasts. Schedules also listed.
- Greek Weather site:
  www.meteo.gr/sailingmapf.asp gives detailed, easy to read wind charts although all text is in Greek.
- Turkish State Meteorological Service:
  www.meteor.gov.tr/indexmaster_eng.htm contains marine forecasts up to 72 hours surface wind and wave heights for the Eastern Med. Good site with text and graphic options.
- Israeli Meteorological Service: www.ims.gov.il

GRIB

A number of sites send GRIB weather files. You will need suitable software to read the files:
Ugrib: www.grib.us
www.passageweather.com
www.globalmarine.net
www.raymarine.com
www.navcenter.com

8 Berthing and Anchoring

Throughout the Mediterranean yachts normally go stern-to (or bows-to) the quay. In a few places you will go alongside, but this is the exception. There are good reasons for berthing Med-style as opposed to alongside:

- It allows more yachts of all sizes to use the quay space available. Each yacht gets its own bit of private quay space to get ashore. If yachts are alongside then you have to clamber over all the inside yachts to get ashore and come back on board. Getting supplies and drunken crew on board is a nightmare and complaints from the inside yachts are inevitable.
- If there is a surge in the harbour, as there often can be, yachts alongside can suffer considerable damage. When you are stern-to you can pull yourself off slightly and stop the boat from damaging itself against the quay.
- You leave when you want to. If you are berthed alongside and there are yachts outside of you, then you will need to make arrangements with them if you want to leave before they do. In bad weather you may be pinned inside a raft of yachts whereas if you are stern-to, you can leave quickly and efficiently at will.
- Berthing Med-style keeps unwanted visitors from gaining easy access to the boat, and I don't just mean the two-legged variety. Cockroaches, rats and cats find it more difficult to get on board when stern-to compared to alongside when they can wander onboard at will. Raise the gang-plank and you effectively have a moat between the shore and your floating castle.
- It is more private. If you are the yacht directly on the quayside then anyone can look in or down the hatches to see what is going on. And all those crew members passing politely across the foredeck to an outside boat will more than likely be passing over the front cabin where you are sleeping with its hatch open for ventilation.

Stern-to

Berthing stern-to for the first time can be a nightmare. There you are, lined up to go between five million dollars worth of motor yacht on one side, and a rusting home-built steel affair that was supposed to go around the world but is now an obstruction bristling with dangerous protuberances. On the quay, people are shouting instructions and on the large motor yacht, grim-faced crew are getting out more fenders the size of mooring buoys. You can't get the yacht to go

Throughout the Mediterranean, yachts normally berth stern-to. Make everything ready before you start; have fenders out and lines coiled for throwing.

astern with that fresh wind on the beam and the engine is starting to overheat. Do you think I'm exaggerating? Trust me, it will get better after the first few attempts. Do not give up and resort to anchoring everywhere, as some circumnavigators do when they arrive in the Med and can't stand the embarrassment of berthing stern-to. Trust your instincts and get a feel for the way the yacht handles and think about how the 12 steps to successful berthing Med-style, given below, relate specifically to your yacht.

Twelve steps to Med-style berthing

1 Make sure you are organised before you get into harbour. Everyone should know what their job is and where everything is. Establish some hand signals for communicating between the person on the anchor and the helmsman rather than trying to shout instructions. There is nothing worse than seeing crews hollering at each other and causing panic on board, not to mention on neighbouring yachts.

2 Have everything ready before you enter harbour. In many harbours there is limited room to manoeuvre and you don't want to be scrambling around getting lines, fenders and the anchor ready. Tie fenders along the widest beam of the boat with the top of the fender on the toe-rail. There is no point in having fenders dangling at the very front and back of the boat except on the quarter, especially on

the leeward side where the wind may push you onto the other boat as you reverse in. We are taught not to tie fenders on the lifelines but, in practice, we all do because fenders can then be positioned in exactly the right place and, more importantly, moved quickly if necessary. If you have enough crew, put someone on the side-deck with a roving fender.

3 Make sure that all lines have been flaked and coiled ready for throwing. One of the areas where crews often lack skill is being able to throw a line properly, so make sure everyone can do so. Lines should be cleated on and then led outside the pushpit and lifelines and into the cockpit, with the free end coiled for throwing. Make sure the line is free of obstructions like the outboard or horseshoe lifebuoy, and double-check it is outside the pushpit and lifelines. Have a spare line handy, flaked and coiled in case it is needed.

4 When you enter harbour, take your time and look around at available berths. Often there will be someone frantically waving you in and shouting instructions. Acknowledge them and then continue doing your own thing. If possible pass close enough to empty spaces to see if there are any obstructions and how deep it is close to the quay. You may find that part of the quay is empty because it is shallow or there is an obstruction in that spot. At the same time, have a look at other anchor rodes to get an idea of where you will drop your anchor without fouling anyone.

5 When choosing a spot, especially when there is a bit of wind about, and the wind is beam-on, try to pick a slot between two yachts where you will be able to slide snugly in and be held in place until you have sorted things out. Alternatively, at least try to find a berth where the prevailing wind will cause you to lie against another yacht – preferably larger than you.

6 You should drop your anchor three to four boat lengths straight out from the chosen vacant spot. If there are yachts on the quay of a similar size to you then estimate three to four lengths out using them as a reference. If in doubt, err on the side of dropping it further out rather than further in. Sometimes people drop their anchor upwind of the berth, which just pulls other people's anchors out or makes it impossible for others to anchor in berths upwind. If you are worried about the holding, wind or swell in a harbour, then drop your anchor further out. *Do not drop it upwind across other anchors.*

7 Most modern yachts go astern easily and you can pretty much forget about the paddle-wheel effect of the propeller once you have some way on. Remember that it takes a little way before a yacht will manoeuvre astern, so start some distance from where you intend to drop the anchor. Once you have steerage way on, do not put the rudder hard over or you will lose steerage because the rudder becomes little more than a brake. Use just a small amount of movement to turn the rudder somewhere between 15 and 20 degrees.

Once you are going astern, keep the boat going and the anchor running freely. A big fender on the transom will help if you overcook things when coming in.

If there is a bit of wind around, try to pick a spot between two yachts where you will be able to slide snugly in.

Once close enough in, throw a line ashore and adjust the lines to get the requisite distance off the quay.

If you have a friendly soul alongside, you may be able to take a line from amidships across to him just to hold the boat in position while you sort out the stern lines.

8 Once the anchor is down, make sure the person laying it out does not snub it until you are nearly in the berth. If the anchor snubs while you are going astern, it will jerk the bows off to one side or the other and you will be pulled off your line and lose steerage way. That means that at all times *the anchor should be allowed to run out freely*. If you have a windlass it is best to release the clutch and let the chain run out under gravity, rather than under power. Most windlasses can't run fast enough to keep pace with the reversing boat, and you will end up with much less chain out than you think you have, as the anchor drags along the bottom. Under gravity, you can always re-engage the clutch to control the rate the chain goes out, and can easily snub the chain when necessary. Once you are about half a boat's length off the quay the anchor can be snubbed and when you have got a line ashore then the anchor rode can be tightened.

9 It is a good idea to have a large fender tied onto the transom at the point where it would hit the quay. It should be securely tied on so it cannot be pushed up or down, and robust enough to prevent damage to the transom. A lot of modern yachts with sugar scoop transoms have some fitted plastic moulding around the vulnerable part of the transom, but it is not usually man enough for the job.

10 If there are just two of you on the boat, and no one ashore ready and willing to help with lines, then once the anchor rode is tight, you can keep the engine ticking over in astern and,

after throwing a line ashore, hop off and make it fast.

11 Lines can be passed through a mooring ring and back to the boat or can be tied off on the quay. Lines led ashore and back to the boat make it easy when leaving, but this means that you will get chafe in the middle of perfectly good lines rather than at the ends, which can be shortened at the end of the season and so are still serviceable. At times you will need to tie off to stubby bollards or a spike in the quay because a line around it and back to the boat would slip off.

12 Leaving a stern-to berth is easy. After letting go the shore-lines, let the anchor winch do the work rather than powering out. If there is a beam wind you may need to put the boat in forward for a bit when clearing other boats so you are not blown across their anchor rodes. It is important, when leaving, to keep an eye out for stray permanent moorings or rope berthing lines from other boats so you do not get them around your propeller or rudder. If any lines are close to the prop or rudder, go into neutral and do not engage forward (or astern) until you are absolutely sure you are clear.

Bows-to

Berthing bows-to is a viable alternative for yachts up to around 40 feet depending on displacement. It is easier than going stern-to, simply because a yacht is more manoeuvrable going forward as opposed to astern. Personally, I do a little of each. In a well-sheltered

When coming in bows-to, it is easier to wriggle your way into a tight berth and you will be less likely to provide amusing entertainment for an interested quayside audience.

harbour with no bad weather imminent I will frequently go bows-to. Once you are set up it is easy to wiggle your way into a tight berth and it gives you a lot more privacy having the cockpit away from the quay. In some places you will need to berth bows-to because underwater ballasting extends out from the quay and damage to the rudder could result from going stern-to. If the holding is a bit suspect, if strong winds are likely to blow across or onto the quay, if there may be wash from other craft (especially ferries or work-boats), then I go stern-to with a decent amount of chain out. Otherwise I go bows-to.

Most of the points in the 12 steps given above are also relevant to going bows-to so I won't repeat them. However, there are some additional tips and hints which can help.

Bows-to tips

1   It is useful to have a permanent set-up for the stern kedge anchor when going bows-to. In its simplest form this can be a bucket tied on the aft deck with the anchor tied onto the pushpit. More sophisticated set-ups have dedicated stowage for the anchor line and chain, a winch or roller on the aft deck, webbing anchor line and a drum to wind it up on, plus an arrangement on the transom to hold the anchor. Whatever you have, it needs to be easy to use and easy to get at if the chain or rope gets tangled up.

2   A Danforth or Fortress anchor is usually best for going bows-to, as these have good holding power in a straight line for less weight. Don't put too much chain on as it will be difficult to stow and deploy. For an

When you are lined up to come in bows-to, drop the kedge off the stern and let it run.

11-metre boat, a 12 kg Danforth with 5 metres of chain or a FX23 6.4 kg Fortress with 3 metres of chain works well. I use an FX23 with 3 metres of chain on my 11-metre 8-ton boat and this has always worked well.

3 Always flake out the anchor line in the cockpit before letting the anchor go or Sod's Law dictates it will get snarled up. Some yachts have a drum mounted on the pushpit with a simple handle on it, and this appears to work well though it does tend to clutter up the pushpit.

4 Before you come in, tie the bitter end on the anchor off, and take the line around a cockpit winch. This way you can surge the line at will when coming in, and as you get close to the quay you can put some weight on the line to slow the boat down. Once the bow lines are ashore and made off, then you can put a couple of turns around the winch and use it to tighten the anchor rode, making sure that the anchor is properly in.

5 When leaving, use a short burst astern to get some way on and then just haul in the line by hand or on a winch. Be very careful not to engage gear after the initial burst astern as it is all too easy to get the line around the prop.

FOULED ANCHORS

A common problem in many harbours is fouling (snagging) the chain of another yacht with your anchor. Unless you intend to go diving to untangle the mess (not healthy in harbours, or if very short-handed), the only thing to do is to haul both lots up. Assuming, that is, you are not tangled up with the anchor and chain of a mini-liner, in which case it is best to be patient and wait for them to leave. Lifting up an anchor and chain that you have hooked can be hard work and it is best not to be too proud and refuse offers of assistance from well-muscled bystanders, because you don't yet know how big it is. If your cable is all chain, use the anchor winch to get it up. If the anchor winch is not powerful enough, you can help it out by attaching a length of line with a running hitch onto the chain and leading it to a mast winch or, if that is not beefy enough, to a cockpit winch.

Once you have brought the offending chain, line or anchor up to the surface, loop a rope under it and bring it back on deck and cleat it off. Then let your own anchor down so that the rope takes the weight of the other gear, and work your anchor free. Once you have retrieved your anchor and cable you can simply release one end of the rope, letting the stranger's tackle go. Don't get your fingers in the way. And don't use a boathook to hold the chain or line as once you have retrieved your own gear the boathook will be impossible to unhook and will almost certainly be dragged to the bottom with the offending chain or line.

If your anchor is fouled, use a rope or an 'anchor thief' to secure the offending chain or rope. There are enough boathooks on the bottom of the Mediterranean harbours already.

If you can find an 'anchor thief' it is well worth buying it. Alternatively, you may be able to get one made. Basically it is a metal hook with a line attached to the end and another lighter line attached halfway around the curve of the hook. Drop it down to hold the chain or line over your anchor and chain and then, once you are free, a sharp tug on the light line will tip the offending line or chain off.

If you haul up another boat's anchor it is only civil to drop it as far out and in as straight a line as possible, so that her crew will not have to re-lay it themselves. With a large anchor over yours, and in windy conditions, this may be impossible and the only thing to do is to mutter apologies as you slink out of harbour.

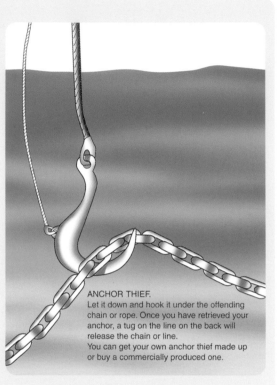

ANCHOR THIEF.
Let it down and hook it under the offending chain or rope. Once you have retrieved your anchor, a tug on the line on the back will release the chain or line.
You can get your own anchor thief made up or buy a commercially produced one.

Dealing with a fouled anchor: Take a line under the offending chain and make it fast at both ends on deck (**1** and **2**). Work your own anchor free (**3**). Retrieve your anchor and let one end of the lifting line go.

Marinas

Using your own anchor to berth stern-to, or bows-to, is by far and away the most common method, but in all marinas and some harbours there will be laid moorings. You still go stern- or bows-to, but using a variety of fixed moorings rather than your anchor, as follows.

- **Line tailed to the quay** Here the mooring line from the mooring block and sinker is tied at its inner end to the quay. Some dexterity with the boathook is required to pick up the line and lead it to your bow or stern (whichever is away from the quay) as quickly as possible. Often a marina attendant will pull the line tight from the quay so you can pick it up more easily. It's not a bad idea to wear gloves as the mooring line may be covered in barnacles and coral worm, which can cause nasty cuts. The mooring line may be a bit too large for a cleat and in that case it is not a bad idea to have a smaller diameter line handy and tie it on to the mooring line – a clove hitch or a running hitch usually works fine.
- **Buoyed lines** In some marinas you must pick up a buoy which has a line leading to a chain sinker and a mooring block on the bottom. This requires some dexterity with a boathook, especially on boats with a high freeboard. Wear gloves to avoid cuts.
- **Posts** In some marinas, especially French ones, you must put two lines onto a post on either side of the berth from your bow or stern (whichever is away from the quay). Tie one to your bow cleat (assuming you are stern-to) and tie the second line to an amidships cleat as a spring (only necessary on the windward side).

The lines to the posts effectively hold you out instead of an anchor. It is much easier to lead a line around the post and have both ends on the boat rather than attempt to tie the bitter end to the post. This also makes leaving the berth much easier.

Once you are safely berthed it is not a bad idea to ask other cruisers around you about the strength of the mooring line and chain, and have a good look yourself, especially for corrosion near the surface, or loss of metal where chain links meet. There have been numerous occasions – too many for complacency – where the line or chain has broken in bad weather. In the event of strong onshore winds it is prudent to lay out your own anchor, but place it far enough away to avoid fouling the permanent mooring blocks and chains, or you may have to pay for a diver to go down and untangle the mess.

Harbour practice and hazards

Although the problems of going stern-to in a crosswind may occupy your mind in harbour, the mechanics of manoeuvring are not the only thing you must watch out for. Lurking inside a harbour are a number of traps that are not always obvious, and you should take a bit of time to look around and make a mental note of potential hazards.

■ **Floating lines** Local fishermen throughout the Mediterranean seem to delight in using polypropylene rope for permanent mooring lines that float on the surface. Often they zigzag all over the place and almost certainly across the course you want to take to a berth. The only way to deal with this menace is to nudge your way in slowly, putting the engine into neutral whenever a line looks like getting anywhere near the keel, rudder or propeller. Station someone on the side-deck with a boathook to try to keep the line away from the boat. Alternatively, find another berth that is not obstructed by a local's mooring line.

■ **Local boats and sailors** Local boats often have macho skippers who like to charge in and out of harbour at full throttle. The bronzed Adonis on the helm will gun his boat out of harbour before throttling down to an economical speed, and likewise will gun her into harbour after pottering back slowly from picking up the nets. Treat local boats with caution when they are coming in and out of harbour and never assume they know the rules of the road. The rule is: you keep out of the way.

■ **Ferries** In the case of ferries, the rule is simply that might is right and again you always keep out of the way. Often they have to perform difficult manoeuvres in a confined space without the aid of a tug, so make sure you give them plenty of room and keep clear.

■ **Local knowledge** In out-of-the-way harbours, locals are often unfamiliar with the anatomy of a yacht and don't realise it has bits sticking down into the water or that rudders and keels extend further than on local boats. Often you will be beckoned into a space by a well-meaning local. When you ask how deep it is, he will roll his eyes and mime that it is deep enough to take a supertanker, and so you edge in, only to run aground. In some instances there will be sufficient depth to get in, but all too often there is not: treat local depths with caution.

Always keep an eye out for ships or ferries when coming into harbour.

THE CAÏQUE MOOR

In Greece the local caïques are notoriously difficult to manoeuvre, especially astern, so the locals use what I call the 'caïque moor' to come in stern-to. It can be useful for long-keel yachts that are difficult to drive astern and I used to use the technique on my previous long-keeled boat. It needs to be stressed here that you should have everything ready and that the person handling the anchor is on the button with the timing to let the anchor go and to snub it.

Basically the caïque moor involves heading towards the berth as if going bows-to and letting the bower anchor go – around four boat lengths out. At this stage, the boat is coasting in with the anchor chain running out

freely. When about two boat lengths out, the chain is snubbed and the boat swings around in a gentle arc until the stern is pointing towards the quay. You then go astern and tie up while everyone applauds your elegant berthing skills. The technique is all about judgement and timing over where to drop the anchor and when to snub it.

The caïque moor can also be used when anchoring normally. Once you have chosen the spot, you coast in downwind and let sufficient chain go before snubbing it and gently swinging around to lie head-to-wind. The technique is useful when sailing into an anchorage as the momentum of the boat digs the anchor in nicely.

The caïque moor is where you approach bows-to and swing round on your bower anchor to berth astern. It is a useful technique if you have a boat that is difficult to drive astern.

- **Close in** In many harbours there are blocks of masonry rubble – old pieces of the quay that fell off some time ago, or chunks of ballast from when it was built – projecting under water or piled up at the base. Some quays also have a step or ledge below the water level, visible only when you are close in. Care must be taken especially when mooring stern-to, or you can damage the rudder or skeg. Going in bows-first lessens the problem. Sometimes there may be no quay at all, but just a rough rock breakwater. The only thing to do in this situation is to moor stern-to or bows-to with a long line ashore. Because you will not be able to get the boat close enough to step off, you will have to use the dinghy to get ashore. Don't be put off mooring like this or you may miss some utterly charming and idyllic fishing harbours.

- **Avoiding damage** If you are rolling around in a crowded berth and rubbing up against the boats on either side, it is worth pulling yourself clear to avoid damage. This is particularly important if boats are rolling, when damage to masts and rigging can occur; adjust lines so that masts and the very vulnerable spreaders and masthead gear do not clash. Squirt detergent on the fenders to stop them squeaking and disturbing your sleep.

Anchors

Talking about anchors is a bit like talking about politics or religion. Everyone has fairly set ideas on what works and why. What follows is necessarily a fairly personal opinion on the different anchors available; in fact many of us tend to use what we already have because anchors are costly to buy and the differences between anchor types are less important than the differences between good and bad anchoring practice. One thing I am quite adamant about is the use of spade-type anchors over Danforth- or Fisherman-type anchors for the main or bower anchor. Any anchor that has flukes sticking out can foul the chain as the boat swings around the anchor and effectively renders it useless. For this reason, I suggest you use any of the spade types for a main anchor and a Danforth-type anchor for a kedge.

Below I give marks out of ten for how effective the different anchors are. It is a purely personal rating from my experience in the Med and I expect the different manufacturers have technical figures that would disagree with my ratings.

Main anchor

Manson (8½) and Rocna (8½) These two New Zealand anchors (available in the UK) seem to win in tests for holding power and re-setting satisfactorily.

Delta (8), Spade (8), SARCA (7) and Bugel (7) These four probably dig in the best, especially through weed, and have the best holding power once in. They also have designs that angle the anchors into the right position to dig in rather than lying on their sides.

CQR (6½) A genuine CQR, with a weighted tip, will generally dig into most ground, although in thick weed and on hard sand you will probably have to have a couple of attempts to get it in.

CQR copy (5) These get a lesser rating because they don't have a weighted tip.

Meon (4½) and Bruce (5) The Meon is an adaptation of big ship anchors and is really only suitable for larger yachts. The Bruce works well in mud but not on sand or rocky bottoms. There is a tendency for the Bruce to get certain-sized rocks stuck between the claws.

Kedge anchor

Fortress (8) Don't ask me why this aluminium anchor works so well, but it provides good holding on most ground, with the bonus of easy handling because of its light weight.

Danforth type (6–7) Depending on the design and length of the flukes, these work well.

Fisherman (5) It needs to be big and heavy and this limits its usefulness. It works well on hard sand and rock.

Grapnel (3) It is OK for a dinghy anchor, but not as the first choice for a kedge.

Anchoring

You will be doing a lot more anchoring in the Med than is common around northern Europe, and even if you are proficient in the art of anchoring, the Mediterranean has some special problems, the biggest being the difficult holding ground you will encounter. There is a lot of talk about how difficult it is to anchor in the Med, but much of it derives from not paying attention to small details. I've been anchoring for 25 years in Med anchorages and while there are places where it is difficult to get the anchor to bite, in most places

good practice, the right gear, and some patience will do the job. The following points should help you to anchor successfully, although all anchoring requires that special nose for sniffing out potential problems and taking action before things spiral out of control.

Anchoring tips

1 Spend some time looking around a new anchorage before you decide where to drop the hook. Look carefully at the chart to see if the bottom slopes gently, or suddenly from a hump. Potter around sounding the depths, and if you can see the bottom, which is possible even in 10 metres or more, look for a weed-free sandy or muddy patch in which to let your anchor down.

2 Always remember that where you drop your anchor is not where you will end up. Mentally plot your swinging circle around the anchor to see how you are going to lie if the wind shifts. Watch how any other craft in the anchorage are lying and look carefully at the type of boat and its anchoring gear. A heavy, deep-draught boat lying to all-chain will tend to swing around the chain, which itself acts as an anchor. A light motorboat on rope will range all over the place in the slightest breeze.

3 While you are checking out the anchorage, it is important to have someone experienced up on the bow where visibility is so much better than from the cockpit. They can effectively assess distances from other boats, and rocks or other dangers, and look down into the water to search out a sandy or muddy patch free of weed.

SECOND ANCHOR OR TANDEM METHOD

There has been a lot of debate over whether to use a second anchor on a separate chain and rope or to use the tandem system.

When laying a second anchor, I usually opt to row it out in the tender. I choose to row rather than use the outboard because if there is a snarl up of any sort, it is easy to keep stationary when rowing as opposed to using an outboard. I usually balance the anchor on the stern of the dinghy so I can kick it over with my foot when I'm in the right place. The crew on the bow of the yacht should pay out the rope so it doesn't impede your rowing nor sink to the bottom or get blown by the wind into a big bight on the water.

When single-handed I've sometimes employed the method of getting the second anchor ready up forward and then motoring up to where I want to drop it. To do this you need to assess exactly where the main anchor is, and then choose a conspicuous transit around 45 degrees off the main rode to aim for when motoring up. It's a matter of judgement to avoid fouling your main anchor and not motoring too far while dragging the chain up.

Many people recommend anchoring using a tandem system, whereby you have two anchors on the same chain; you attach the second anchor about 5–10 metres back from the main anchor. The idea is that the second anchor acts as a sort of super-snubber: holding the chain down for the main anchor and also digging in itself to provide extra holding power. Personally, I think it is a clumsy system which takes ages to deploy and retrieve. If the tandem system doesn't hold, it can be difficult to get out of a dangerous situation quickly; only this year I had to help a yacht employing the tandem system, which went onto rocks after the two anchors dragged and the skipper couldn't get the whole affair on board quickly enough. I think laying a second anchor provides more security and is more easily handled if things do go wrong. That said, the tandem system does have fans who swear by it.

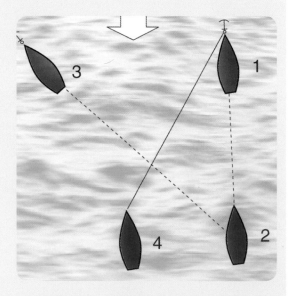

Laying a second anchor from the boat. Motor up at an angle of 45 degrees to the main anchor; drop the second anchor and fall back on the two anchors.

Pre-arranged hand signals will enable the person in the bow to select a spot with adequate swinging room, clear of other boats, and position the anchor over a sandy or muddy patch. There is nothing that disturbs an anchorage more than a boat coming in with the skipper and crew arguing and shouting at one another, and nothing so pleasing as a boat that carries out the whole operation in a quiet and seamanlike manner.

4 One of the biggest problems with anchoring in the Mediterranean is weed. The eel grasses, *Zostera marina* and *Cymodocea nodosa*, and Neptune grass, *Posidonia nodosa*, grow prolifically, forming underwater meadows that can be well over a metre thick in places, though usually less. These grasses grow close together and their fibrous roots and branching rhizomes stop an anchor penetrating and digging into the sea bottom. Quite often an anchor will pick up a clump of weed on its point, which clogs it completely. When this happens, the only thing to do is haul it up and clear the weed off, otherwise it simply will not set – no matter how much scope you lay out.

In some areas damage to Posidonia from yachts anchoring and ploughing it up has given rise to environmental concerns. Posidonia is home to a wide range of marine organisms and ploughing through it disturbs the habitat. Moorings have been laid in some areas of concern and these should be used where available. It is likely that in the future more areas will have moorings and that a

One of the problems you will encounter when anchoring in the Med is dense beds of weed such as eel grass. If your anchor hooks up a clump, the only thing to do is to lift it and pull the weed off, otherwise the anchor will not set.

charge will be made for using them.

5 In other places, you will come across hard sand where it is difficult to get the anchor to dig in. There is not too much you can do except be patient and try again. The pilot book or other cruisers should tell you if there is hard sand or, as is sometimes the case, a thin layer of sand over rock. In both these conditions it is useful if you can dive down to set the anchor by hand. Otherwise just persevere and set a second anchor if necessary.

6 Another problem is that you must often anchor in fairly deep water. Many anchorages do not slope gently up to the shore but instead rise abruptly from 10 or 15 metres. For this reason some yachts carry a combination of chain and rope to make anchor handling easier; even some electric anchor winches have difficulty pulling up the combined weight of an anchor and its all-chain

Anchoring with a long line ashore is standard practice in many parts of the Mediterranean.

cable when it is straight up and down in 15 or 20 metres or more. Biceps have even more trouble. In difficult holding ground, with a layer of weed on the bottom, depth also adds to the problem of getting an anchor to dig in and hold properly. There is no easy solution to this; let as much chain and rope out as possible to ensure a semi-horizontal pull on the anchor rope and keep at it until you are certain it is set well in. Remember to let the anchor and chain down by releasing the clutch so that gravity does the work rather than your winch and battery. Letting an anchor down under power is not only wasting your amps, but is also too slow to let chain down onto the bottom.

7 Setting an anchor is a skill that requires a certain amount of practice in areas with poor holding. Once the chain (and rope) has been laid out, go slowly astern until you feel the anchor bite. You can see when it happens by watching the chain or rope, which will come up taut and stay taut rather than jerking through

In the eastern Mediterranean you will often find restaurants that have built a rough catwalk or quay, often with laid moorings. If you use this facility, it is only politic to eat at the restaurant.

the water. It is essential you do not put too much throttle on when powering astern and you should go into neutral a few times so you can get the anchor to bite. It's a bit like fishing – just give a tug on the line to turn the anchor over and start it digging in rather than ploughing a furrow through the bottom. Once you feel the anchor has taken hold, gradually put the revs up in astern to about half cruising revs, watching the chain and your position relative to the other boats in the anchorage

and the shore to see if the anchor is really holding. Motoring astern like this may sound a little extreme, but if you don't do this, you won't know if the anchor is set or not. It is all too easy for the anchor to hook on a thick clump of weed and appear to be holding, only to have the wind change direction or strength and dislodge it – probably when you are ashore with a drink in your hand. With rope you will have to watch more closely to see that it comes up tight and stays like that as you are going astern.

121

An anchor snubber (just a short length of rope will do) will stop the anchor chain rumbling over the roller and it also takes the strain off the anchor winch.

8 To double check, while the boat is going astern, hold the chain or rope lightly with your hand and you will be able to feel whether the anchor is bumping over the bottom or holding, via the vibrations travelling up the chain or rope. However, do not confuse the chain bumping over the bottom as it straightens out with the anchor dragging: it takes a little experience to be able to feel just what is happening down there.

9 If you are worried about the holding, or the weather, don't hesitate to lay a second anchor. All too often I have been in an anchorage where things have been a bit iffy and have hopped in the dinghy to lay a second anchor, even though conditions did not really justify it. Almost immediately, other yachts' skippers around me who have been debating whether or not to lay a second anchor have hopped into their dinghies to do the same. It takes little time to lay a second anchor but

it means you rest easy even if the weather does not warrant it.

10 A trip line attached to the crown of the anchor and a small floating buoy is sometimes useful when anchoring on rocky bottoms where the anchor can get wedged. The line should be about the same length as the depth you are anchoring in. Too short and the buoy will be submerged; too long and there will be loops of line in the water which can get fouled.

Some people employ a similar system in crowded anchorages, just so that others can identify where their anchor is. Personally I think this an unnecessary and somewhat selfish practice. It severely restricts the amount of room in the anchorage, as the floating buoy creates an additional hazard which your own swinging circle must avoid. The other downside is that if you drift over your own buoy as the wind changes you may foul your rudder or propeller.

ANCHORING WITH A LONG LINE ASHORE

In some parts of the Mediterranean (in Turkey for example, where you must anchor in deep water on an upward slope) the practice has evolved of taking a line ashore to a bollard or rock, or tree if neither of the other options is available. The prevailing winds in summer are constantly from the same direction and you will normally be taking the line ashore to 'anchor' the boat against an offshore wind and also to hold the anchor in place in the uphill-sloping seabed. If you were to swing around the anchor it would be pulled downhill and into deeper water. This manoeuvre is usually carried out using the main bower anchor and tying ashore from the stern.

When you are anchoring in this fashion, have the dinghy in the water and ready to go with a long line – you will often need 50 or 60 metres – flaked down in the dinghy and the end tied off on the boat. Drop the anchor and go astern until you are positioned where you want to be off the shore. Once the anchor is in, you should be able to hold the boat in position with the engine idling astern while the person in the dinghy rows like fury to the shore. Some care is needed (especially if things start to go wrong) to avoid the line getting anywhere near the propeller. If you have a strong swimmer on board it may be possible to swim a line ashore over a short distance, but a length of line in the water soon becomes very heavy to tow. Also ensure that the swimmer has footwear to protect his feet from sea urchins and sharp rocks near the shore.

If an anchorage is very crowded, or you are in a cove with no swinging room and it is impossible to get a line ashore, you will have to anchor fore-and-aft. Have a look around the spot you are going to occupy and then motor upwind and drop the main anchor. Fall back on this and, if necessary, tie a length of extra rope to it so you can get back far enough to let the second anchor go over the stern. It is then a matter of adjusting the two until you are happy with the way you are lying, and satisfied that both anchors are in and holding. Anchoring fore-and-aft can be useful where the water gradually becomes shallow, as you can position yourself in a spot where swinging to an anchor would not work.

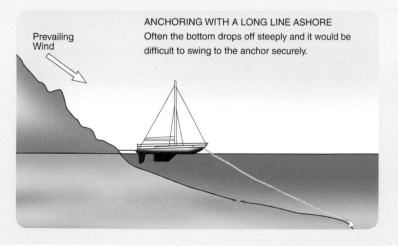

ANCHORING WITH A LONG LINE ASHORE
Often the bottom drops off steeply and it would be difficult to swing to the anchor securely.

Prevailing Wind

This is a very abbreviated guide to getting around the Mediterranean. The order of the different countries is clockwise around the Med, and the descriptions more or less follow the same format:

Cruising area and description

Brief description of the coast and cruising area.

Cruising routes

Main cruising routes around the coast and to or from other countries. Apart from 'local' routes described under the country information, there are a few longer Med routes that are described here.

MED 1 Gibraltar along the coast of North Africa

This is the shortest passage to the eastern Mediterranean and is also a busy shipping route between the Suez Canal and the Atlantic. Although there is a favourable east-going current along the North African coast, there is often little wind, or contrary wind in places. It must also be remembered that, for 560 miles or so along the Algerian coast, you are close to a country that has some civil unrest and consequently the authorities may be suspicious of small craft sailing along their coast. The route is used by some large motorboats on delivery, but a few sailing yachts also come this way.

Once up to the Sicilian Strait and Malta you can continue on MED 2 or cross to the Adriatic or Greece (see relevant sections).

MED 2 Sicilian Strait and Malta to Port Said

This the quick route from the western Mediterranean to Port Said to transit the Suez Canal. In the summer, the prevailing wind is westerly or north-westerly, although in practice wind directions in this part of the Mediterranean can be variable and there will often be little wind except closer to the coast. In spring and autumn, some care is needed as depressions often track across the Gulf of Sidre and into the south-eastern Mediterranean. Although small, these depressions can be intense with strong winds which whip up considerable seas. Care is also needed on this route because of the amount of shipping between the Suez Canal and the Atlantic.

MED 3 Greece and Cyprus to Israel and Port Said

From Greece, most yachts will leave from Rhodes or Crete for Cyprus or Port Said. For either destination the prevailing winds blowing from the north-west will be favourable although once 30–50 or so miles to the south-east, the *meltemi* will be lost and at night it is likely to be calm.

From Cyprus, yachts can head for Haifa (Quishon Marina) or Herzilia or Ashkelon further south. Remember it is imperative to call the Israeli Navy on VHF Ch16 when 20 miles out. The distance from Cyprus to Port Said is around 240 miles so it is better to leave at midday or early afternoon and allow for two nights out. Yachts on passage up the Red Sea, and arriving in Port Said in March or April, should keep an eye out for depressions whipping across the south-eastern corner of the Mediterranean as they can be unusually fierce at times (even after the Red Sea). On all these passages you will need to keep a good look-out for shipping between the Red Sea and the Dardanelles.

Distance tables
See Appendix 3 giving distance tables for western and central Mediterranean.

Weather and seasons
A brief resumé of the climate and seasons and details of prevailing winds and strong winds to watch out for.

Formalities
Paperwork for clearing in and out.

Ashore
What to expect ashore in the way of provisioning, markets, restaurants, and bars.

Yacht facilities
Boatyards and marinas including popular lay-up yards and marinas for over-wintering.

Airports
An indication of low cost and charter flights into and out of a country for crew changes, visitors, or returning home for the winter.

Shoestring cruising
A brief round-up of ways to get around a country on a budget. This is an instance where something that looks like an extravagance, a mobile phone, can save you money if you phone ahead to a marina to check up on price. I regularly do this and it works a treat. The other thing the cruiser on a budget must do is to check in pilots or any other publications for current charges. In my pilots and the *Mediterranean Almanac* (Imray). I give charge bands for different marinas, but these are necessarily researched anything from 6 months to a year or more before publication. The charge band system is as follows:

For a 12-metre yacht (high season)
Charge band 1 No charge
Charge band 2 Low cost (under 25 euros)
Charge band 3 Medium cost (26–40 euros)
Charge band 4 Medium–high cost (41–55 euros)
Charge band 5 High cost (56–70 euros)
Charge band 6 Very high cost (71–100 euros)
Charge band 6+ Over 100 euros

Reading
Here I list only books relevant to sailing. You should of course carry lots of other guide books. For culture buffs most of the *Blue Guides* from Somerset Books can be relied upon although they can be stodgy at times. The *Rough Guides* and *Lonely Planet Guides* are OK, but always remember that a restaurant or

bar recommended by one of these guides becomes overwhelmed by people eager to eat or drink there. There are also lots of local guide books and one-off books that can give you a good insight into a place and maybe a good read as well. For these you will have to do your own research.

GIBRALTAR

'The Rock' is instantly recognisable in the western approaches to the Mediterranean. It has been quarrelled over, fought over and the subject of bitter referendums. In 2006 Britain, Gibraltar and Spain signed an agreement to improve relations between the latter two countries. Flights between Spain and Gibraltar have now resumed, after a 30-year gap. It has good facilities for yachts and is an ideal stepping off point into the Atlantic or a first Mediterranean destination going east. Gibraltar is more of a stopover for boats entering or leaving the Mediterranean than a cruising area, and boats based here cruise the adjacent Spanish coast or cross to Morocco just 14 miles away.

Cruising routes

There are two important routes into and out of Gibraltar:

ATL1 From the Atlantic into the Strait of Gibraltar

Yachts coming from the Azores or from the Atlantic Coast of Spain will generally make the approach along or towards the Spanish coast from Cabo Trafalgar. From the Azores (around 1000 miles), yachts will often have had a bumpy passage and

the approach to the Strait is normally a relief except if strong easterlies are blowing and in anticipation of these, cruisers should have a number of ports of refuge in mind. Cádiz is useful as it can be entered in all weather and has a good deep water channel. A bit further south, Barbate is also useful. If you are coming up to the Strait of Gibraltar and find adverse wind and tide then you can anchor behind Isla de Tarifa. It is very windy here but the holding is pretty good. In the approaches, and the Strait itself, you will come across much shipping and it is imperative you keep a good lookout and radar watch if possible. You may also encounter fog which is surprisingly common in the early morning from April to May.

ATL2 From Gibraltar to the Canaries (around 800 miles)

Yachts leaving for the Canaries will be able to pick a weather window that will, hopefully, give a good passage. They should plan the passage out of the Straits with some care. Yachts entering the Straits have fewer possibilities for timing and my advice in or out is to stick close to the northern side where, apart from being out of the shipping channels, you have a better chance of picking up a favourable stream, and at least encounter less tide and current against you. Yachts normally leave anywhere from September to November and should experience north-north-easterly winds around 15–25 knots at this time. The later you leave, the more likely the chance that depressions will pass through – often spawning south-westerly gales. With gales in this sea area, it should be

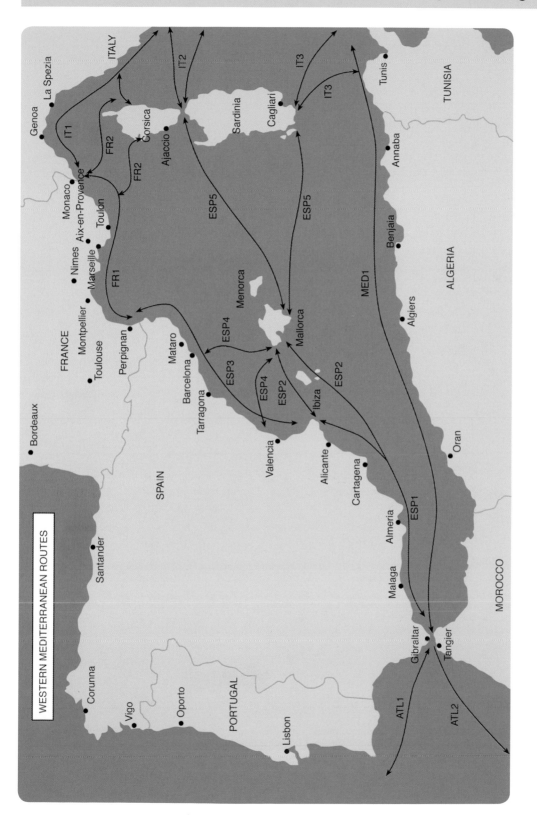

WESTERN MEDITERRANEAN ROUTES

Looking down from 'the Rock' over the marinas and runway at Gibraltar towards La Linea in Spain. There is now a new marina at La Linea which is an alternative to Gibraltar.

remembered that large swells pile up on the Moroccan Atlantic coast and few harbours are safe to enter – with the exception of Casablanca and possibly Safi and Agadir. Yachts should try to get offshore and weather any gales there rather than approach the Moroccan coast where there have been a number of fatal accidents. Some yachts head for Madeira, then south to the Canaries. Landfall in the Canaries is usually at Graciosa, Lanzarote or Gran Canaria.

Weather and seasons

Winds are mainly from the east (*levanter*) or the west (*vendevale*). Either wind is channelled through the Strait so that while you might have 15 knots, 10–15 miles either side, in the Strait itself you can have 25–40 knots. With a near-gale and a wind-against-tide situation in the Strait, some care is needed.

The climate in Gibraltar is mild all year round although Atlantic depressions can seep in, bringing rain and fog.

Formalities

Yachts can now complete clearing-in procedures from whichever marina they are in. Gibraltar is a full member of the EU though it has special exemptions to EU regulations concerning customs, VAT or RCD for yachts.

Ashore

Gibraltar has always been a favourite port for yachts provisioning with English commodities. There is a supermarket (Morrisons) with a good selection of UK-branded goods at reasonable prices. Ashore there are a number of restaurants of different flavours ranging from basic English including fish and chips to quasi-Mediterranean. Bars in Gib range from fairly plush affairs all the way through to some delightfully seedy back-street jobs.

Yacht facilities

Gibraltar has facilities for most yacht repairs including mechanical, engineering, electrical, electronic and servicing work. What it does not have is a lot of hardstanding. Sheppards has a chandlery and there are a number of other marine-related shops. Goods can be sent duty free to Gibraltar.

Airports

Gibraltar Airport is next to the border. Reasonably priced scheduled flights to the UK are available. Alternatively, you can get charter or low cost scheduled flights from Malaga.

Shoestring cruising

Marina Bay is charge band 2. Queensway is charge band 3. Yachts can anchor off on the Spanish side off La Linea if permitted off the new marina, as technically, anchoring off Gibraltar (off the runway) is now prohibited.

Reading

Imray Mediterranean Almanac, edited by Rod Heikell and Lucinda Heikell, Imray.

SPAIN

Mediterranean Spain has a fairly straight coastline some 750 miles long (without counting too many bumps) running north-east from Gibraltar to the Gulf of Lions. Around 50 miles offshore are the

129

Almerimar on the Costa del Sol is a popular spot for wintering over.

Balearic Islands, which is probably the most popular sailing area with a large number of marinas and resident yachts. The mainland coast is traditionally cut up into chunks which from Gibraltar are the Costa del Sol (175 miles), Costa Blanca (200 miles), Costa del Azahar (125 miles), Costa Dorada (160 miles), and Costa Brava (90 miles). Large parts of the coast have developments of hotels and marina-apartment complexes, with the Costa del Sol and Costa Dorada the most built up of the coasts. There are still some small fishing harbours and a number of anchorages, although the coast does not have a lot of natural indentations like the *rías* on the Spanish Atlantic coast.

Cruising routes

ESP1 Coasting from Gibraltar along the mainland coast to around Cabo San Antonio

There are plenty of marinas and harbours along this stretch of coast and at no time will you be more than 40 miles from the next harbour. In places there are harbours every 10–15 miles. The prevailing winds are easterlies although they have a thermal component and consequently there is often a calm in the morning and later the sea breeze kicks in. Watch for the *tramontane* and *mestrale* which blow strongly from the north-northwest.

ESP2 From the Spanish coast anywhere between Almeria and Valencia to the Balearics

Yachts intending to cross to the Balearics from the Spanish coast between Almeria and Valencia can leave at night after the sea breeze dies down and motor pretty much until midday the following day to avoid the onshore winds. At night you may be lucky to pick up enough of a land breeze close to the coast to sail through the night. Keep an eye on Atlantic depressions coming in towards Gibraltar or over the Atlantic coast of France where the latter can give rise to a *tramontana* or a *mistral* if cold air pours through the Toulouse Gap or down the Rhône Valley.

ESP3 Coasting from Cabo San Antonio around the coast and into the Gulf of Lions

As for ESP1 there are marinas and harbours all along this coast and nowhere will you be more than 40 miles from the next harbour and in most cases significantly less. Prevailing winds are easterlies but you have more chance of a *tramontana* or *mistral* kicking up bad weather along here.

ESP4 Costa Brava to the Balearics

Most yachts cross from Barcelona, or nearby, to Palma (about 100 miles). As for ESP2 keep an eye on Atlantic depressions that might cause a tramontana or mistral to sweep down onto the Balearics from the north-east, with strong winds and considerable seas.

ESP5 Balearics and routes east towards Corsica and Sardinia

Routes around the Balearics are straightforward with short distances between marinas or harbours. Routes east towards Corsica (usually to the Strait of Bonifacio) or Sardinia (usually to somewhere like Carloforte at the southern end) need to be planned carefully, watching what is happening to the weather and paying special attention to depressions coming off the Atlantic. It can be all too easy to get caught by a depression that speeds up and enters the Mediterranean or passes over France or North Africa giving bad weather in this exposed stretch of water. Don't underestimate the seas that bad weather can generate in the area between the Balearics, Corsica and Sardinia.

Weather and seasons

Settled conditions around the Spanish coast generally set in around May and extend to September. Because the coast runs south-west to north-east, conditions at the more southerly end can vary significantly from the northern end. Around the Balearics and Costa Brava it pays to be careful in the early and late season when there is every chance of a strong *tramontana* or *mistral* coming out of the Gulf of Lions.

The prevailing wind is the *brisa de mar* which blows from a general easterly direction, though it can vary between north-east and south-east, depending on the slant of the coast and the local topography. It blows fairly consistently over the Balearics from the east to south-east. Generally it blows between 10–20 knots and dies down in the evening. Bad weather usually comes from depressions passing through with the *tramontana* and *mistral* being common in the winter, when they can blow up to force 9–10.

Formalities

Spain as a member of the EU does not require other EU yachts to clear in or out. You may be asked for your papers, and Customs and the Coastguard may make spot checks. Through the Strait of Gibraltar and offshore from the Costa del Sol, it is common to be buzzed by Coastguard helicopters or patrol boats.

Ashore

In any of the cities or large towns there are hypermarkets where you can buy pretty much everything you need. The only problem with these is that they are quite often outside the central town area where you are berthed. Inside the towns you will generally find medium-sized supermarkets with most things and everywhere there are small grocery shops. The Spanish still frequent their small shops so you will find butchers, bakers and delicatessens in most places. Spanish produce is excellent and, of course, their hams and salamis are renowned.

Eating out in Spain is a delight, as long as you avoid the ubiquitous steak and chips fare offered by restaurants in many of the larger resorts. Most Spanish restaurants will have a *menu del día* (set menu) with an interesting choice of dishes including, inevitably, *paella*. A good *paella* takes time to cook so if you see it arriving instantly at another table avoid it. *Tapas* bars can be found in most places and a good local *tapas* bar will have excellent food at cheap prices.

Andraitx in the Balearics.

Yacht facilities

Most large marinas will have a travel hoist, hardstanding and a wide range of services available. In popular areas like Palma in the Balearics, or Barcelona, you may have problems negotiating a haul-out because the yards are fully booked; but in most places yachts up to 15 metres can usually be fitted in.

If you are wintering afloat, there are a number of popular marinas. That said, over time allegiances change and what was popular one year may become less so in other years as live-aboards migrate to other marinas. Bear in mind that a six-month winter contract is often negotiable and it is worth getting in touch, in advance, with marinas to see if a deal can be put together. The following marinas have been popular places to winter afloat in recent years: Estepona, Almerimar, Torrevieja, Altea, Palma de Mallorca, Mahón, Port Vell (Barcelona).

If you are hauling for the winter, a number of marina/yards are popular, although for many, price is the issue and so it depends on what sort of deal is negotiated. Some of the marinas popular for overwintering are also popular for hauling. The following marina/yards have been popular in recent years: Sotogrande, Estepona, Almerimar, Alicante, Jávea, Valencia, Torredembarra, Vilanova Y La Geltru, Aiguadolc, Ginesta, El Masnou, Marina Palamós, Ampuriabrava.

Airports

Low cost airlines fly regular flights through the summer and winter to: Malaga, Almeria, Murcia, Alicante,

Ibiza, Palma (Mallorca), Mahón (Menorca) and Barcelona. Holiday companies also fly to these airports in the summer with some winter flights as well. In general, finding a flight into or out of Spain is not too much of a problem as it remains a popular summer and winter destination.

Shoestring cruising

Most marinas along the coast and around the Balearics start high-season charges on 1 June and these continue through to 1 Oct. Some now have a mid-season price starting in April running to June. That means that you will need to cruise very early or late in the season to avoid high-season charges. Around the Balearics and parts of the mainland, high-season marina charges are some of the most expensive in the Med and even out of season can be very expensive if, that is, you can find a berth. Given the vagary of the weather early and late in the season, this may mean that you end up staying longer in marinas than you intended if bad weather threatens. Some marinas have now started high-season charges from 1 May and this really does push early-season cruising into the possible bad weather zone. The only alternative is to study the yachtsman's pilots and look on the internet to see if there is a site for charges and try to plan your cruising accordingly. Bear in mind that the low-charge band from one season when the pilot was researched may suddenly be substantially increased in another season.

There are few really safe anchorages along the mainland Spanish coast or around the Balearics. Some of these anchorages now have moorings in them and you will be charged for picking them up. In areas like Cabrera in the Balearics, I have no problem with the conservation issues being addressed by permanent moorings, but in other places mooring charges seem very excessive for what is offered. One good thing is that, given the numbers of marinas along the coast, you can often anchor off in what may be an iffy anchorage in a bight or cove and if the weather should turn nasty you don't have to go too far to find a safe harbour.

In general, you can coast-hop along most of the mainland shores and find marinas that lie in charge band 3 or the bottom end of 4. In general the Costa del Sol has the cheapest marinas and the Balearics the most expensive. In Mallorca, the marinas can be very expensive (often charge band 5 or 6) and you need to plan carefully. Menorca has a good mix of anchorages and relatively inexpensive marinas and, to my mind, is more pleasant than Mallorca in the high season.

Reading

RCC Mediterranean Spain: Costas del Sol and Blanca, Robin Brandon/John Marchment, Imray.
RCC Mediterranean Spain: Costas del Azahar, Dorada and Brava, Robin Brandon/John Marchment, Imray.
RCC Islas Baleares, Robin Brandon/Graham Hutt, Imray.
Imray Mediterranean Almanac, edited by Rod Heikell, Imray.
Guia del Navegante España e Portugal, Libreria de Nautica. Available locally in Spain.

Menton on the French Riviera.

FRANCE

France has a relatively short Mediterranean coastline of around 350 miles long, with the off-lying island of Corsica adding about the same length of coastline once you circumnavigate it. Along the short mainland coast, there are more marinas packed in than anywhere else in the Mediterranean. This may give the impression of a nightmare coast lined with buildings from one end to the other. In reality it is not like that and you would do well to remember that parts of the French coast have been developed from the 18th and 19th centuries with the sort of architecture that compares favourably with our bland, reinforced concrete developments. Corsica is a world away and is still a beautiful and savage place.

Cruising routes

FR1 French Mediterranean coast

Around the French coast you are never far from a marina or harbour, and the longest passage you will have to make is just over 30 miles around the mouth of the Rhône. For all intents and purposes, you can sail around the coast and choose where you will end up for the night. Some care is needed in the Gulf of Lions where onshore winds can make the entrances to some marinas dangerous, and a weather eye needs to be kept open for the *tramontane* and *mistral*.

FR2 Crossing to Corsica

Most yachts proceed to somewhere between Toulon and the Riviera ports to make the crossing, which will be something over 100 miles, depending on

Port Miou on the Provencal coast.

your point of departure. You need to have a good weather window because, although the crossing is relatively short, bad weather can quickly blow out of the Gulf of Lions or across from the Gulf of Genoa. Most yachts will head for somewhere like Calvi or St Florent on the north coast or Macinaggio or Bastia on the east coast, though there is no reason why you cannot sail as far as Ajaccio or Bonifacio.

Weather and seasons

In France, the summer settled weather period is fairly similar to Spain, starting around May and extending to the end of September. The exception is the Gulf of Lions which has the highest incidence of gales in the Mediterranean (13 per cent) and is an area to be treated with every caution. Even in early and late season, and at times in the summer, you can get a *mistral* or *tramontane* blowing at gale force, or above, into the gulf. If you are crossing the Gulf of Lions, make sure you have a good weather window as the chances are that if a *mistral* or *tramontane* blows out of the gulf, you will not be able to beat up to a port of refuge. Around the Côte d'Azur and Riviera, the prevailing wind in the summer is a sea breeze blowing from the south-east onto the coast. At times it can get up to force 5–6, but mostly it will be force 3–4.

Corsica is very exposed to wind and sea from all directions and, in general, has more moderate to strong winds in the summer than the mainland coast. With a *mistral*, heavy seas are pushed onto the western coast and a *libeccio* or *tramontane* from Italy also pushes considerable

135

seas onto it. Cap Corse has a deserved reputation for bad weather and winds are funnelled into the Strait of Bonifacio and consequently increase in strength.

Formalities

France, as a member of the EU, does not require other EU yachts to clear in or out. You may be asked for your papers and Customs and the Coastguard may make spot checks, but on average you are unlikely to be troubled for your papers when cruising here.

Ashore

It hardly needs to be mentioned that French produce is outstanding and the French make a virtue of daily markets in almost every town that has more than a few thousand souls. French markets are fascinating and offer bargains to hard-pressed British consumers. Nearly everywhere has grocers, bakers and butchers, not to mention *patisseries* and *charcuteries*, but large supermarkets are often on the outskirts in the *zone industriale* and you will usually need a taxi to get to them.

Eating out in France is a delight, and many restaurants will have a *Prix Fixe* menu with two or three courses for 15–25 euros. At times you wonder how they can provide such good food for the price. The French are serious about food, often pompously so, but you should indulge this national hobby, and take advantage of all the excellent food and wine on offer.

Yacht facilities

Most large marinas will have a travel hoist, hardstanding and a wide range of services available. Around the Riviera and the Côte d'Azur, some yards will fill up quickly and in places like Antibes, which have specialist services and limited hardstanding, you may have difficulty getting a slot. Prices, on average, are cheaper around Languedoc-Rousillon and Provence than further east around the Riviera.

If you are wintering afloat, a number of marinas are popular. As mentioned before, what was a popular place one year is not always the current flavour, and people want different things in the winter depending on inclination and taste. A berth in the middle of bustling downtown Nice may not suit those who prefer somewhere quiet and intimate. Unlike Spain, there are fewer deals to be done for a winter contract in France, but it is worth a go and some less popular marinas may give you a discount off the quoted price. The following marinas have been popular places to winter afloat in recent years: Sète, Martigues, Marseille, Ile des Embiez, Toulon, Grimaud, La Napoule, Antibes and Nice. Shallow-draught yachts also go up into the canals with places like Carcassonne, Port-la-Robine, Le Somail and Capestang on the Canal du Midi being popular, although really you can choose almost anywhere. Check to see that there are no *chômages* (lock closures for maintenance) scheduled for your stay.

If you are hauling for the winter, a number of marina/yards are popular and again it depends on what sort of deal can be negotiated. The following marina/yards have been popular in recent years. Any of the large marina complexes around the coast of Languedoc-Rousillon but especially St Cyprien-Plage, Port Leucate, Gruissan-Neuf and Port Camargue. Most of these places close down for the winter and are ghost towns until the spring, but you can often do very good deals. Other popular places are Port Napoleon, Port à Sec at Martigues, La Ciotat, Toulon, Hyères, St-Raphaël (Santa Lucia), and St-Laurent du Var. Sete and Port Napoleon are popular choices for yachts re-stepping their masts after coming down to the Med through the canals or by truck. On Corsica, Macinaggio and Porto Vecchio have been mentioned.

Airports

Low cost airlines fly regular flights through the summer to Perpignan, Carcassonne, Montpellier, Marignane, Toulon and Nice. Charter flights also fly to these destinations during the summer, as well as to Bastia, Calvi, Ajaccio and Figari on Corsica. Remember the TGV provides a lightning-quick rail connection to Marseille, Toulon and Nice.

Shoestring cruising

In France, as in Spain, most marinas start high season charges on 1 June through to 1 Oct. A few have started charging from 1 May, but this is not common. As a general rule, marinas get more expensive as you go east with those around Languedoc-Rousillon the cheapest and the marinas in east Côte d'Azur and the Riviera the most expensive. Even in high season, many marinas have reasonable charges and if

Cargese on the west coast of Corsica.

you study the charge bands for different marinas you can berth quite economically.

Although there are not a huge number of good anchorages, it is surprising how much of the coast you can visit and find anchorages and *calanques*, which if not always comfortable, are at least tenable in settled weather. The large number of marinas and harbours in close proximity mean that you can leave an anchorage if bad weather threatens and find somewhere close by to pop into. I've cruised much of the coast, stopping in anchorages and occasionally going into marinas. French yachtsmen are adept at anchoring in the lee of a marina breakwater, conditions permitting. You will often find that anchorages are busy by day, but at night the locals all return to their home marina and the anchorages become much less crowded.

In Corsica, marinas tend to charge high prices during the summer period to make up for the dearth of yachts at any other time. Cruise early or late in the season and you will find that the place is relatively deserted and marina charges are not high. Around Corsica there are a large number of well-sheltered anchorages and an even larger number that can be used with care, depending on the wind and sea.

Reading
Mediterranean France and Corsica, Rod Heikell, Imray.
RCC Corsica and Sardinia, Robin Brandon/John Marchment, Imray.
Reeds Mediterranean Almanac, Adlard Coles Nautical.
Imray Mediterranean Almanac, edited by Rod Heikell, Imray.

MONACO

Monaco is a small autonomous enclave on the Riviera. There are two marinas, though unless you have booked you are unlikely to get into Port de Monaco and the best bet is to head for Fontvieille. Along the short coastline of Monaco it is prohibited to anchor off and in any case it is mostly too deep as the bottom drops off abruptly.

If you cannot or do not want to go to Monaco on the water, there are nearby French marinas where you can leave the boat and take a bus or train to this little monarchy.

ITALY

The Italian peninsula, jutting into the Mediterranean for some 500 miles, so closely resembles a leg with a boot on it that it is common to talk of the toe and heel of Italy. It is bordered by a number of seas which, going anticlockwise from the west, include the Ligurian Sea, the Tyrrhenian Sea, the Ionian Sea (off the toe and boot) and the Adriatic on the east coast. On the western side, Italy encompasses Sardinia and Sicily, two of the largest islands in the Mediterranean, as well as numerous small archipelagos lying close to the coast.

The coast varies dramatically from region to region. Much of it is mountainous, where depths are considerable a short distance off the shore, while in other places, most notably along much of the eastern seaboard, the coast is low-lying with shallows extending some distance seawards.

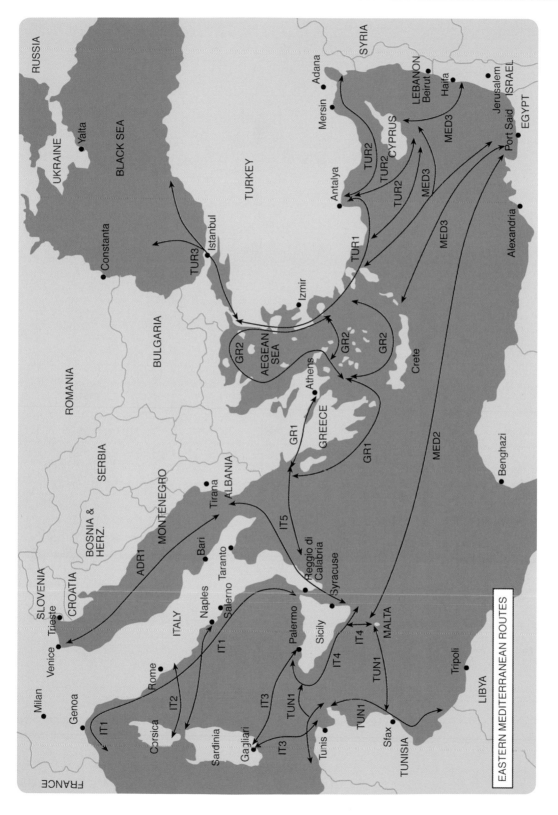

EASTERN MEDITERRANEAN ROUTES

Acciaroli on the coast of Campania. Hemingway is said to have described it as his favourite place in Italy.

The coast is usually divided up into the following areas:

The Italian Riviera Stretching from the French border around to Tuscany, the Riviera has numerous marinas providing every facility. This is geographically and architecturally a beautiful coast, providing much high class cruising.

The Tuscan archipelago and adjacent coast There are a mix of anchorages, harbours and marinas here. It gets crowded in the summer.

The Tyrrhenian seaboard This area stretches from above Rome down to the Strait of Messina. The harbours close to Rome are perennially full of local yachts, but south of Naples the coast is comparatively little frequented except for the off-lying islands, which tend to be popular in the summer.

Sardinia and Sicily Northern Sardinia is popular, but the rest of the island is little cruised apart from in August. It is an exquisite cruising ground, especially around the Strait of Bonifacio. Sicily, once seen as the 'sad-sack' of the islands, now competes with Sardinia in terms of high-season prices, but it has a lot to offer and I, for one, love cruising the coast.

The Ionian sea The area from the toe to the heel is considered not so much a cruising ground as a stepping stone to the Adriatic and Greece, although it is enjoyed by many people.

The Adriatic coast With few attractive harbours and anchorages (Venice excepted), this area is not a popular cruising ground. Most yachtsmen choose to cruise in Croatian waters on the opposite side of the Adriatic.

Cruising routes

IT1 French border to Strait of Messina

Like on the French coast, you are never far from a marina or harbour and the longest passages you will have to make are 30–35 miles between places like Livorno and Elba, Monte Argentario and Civitavecchia, Gaeta and Ischia, Maratea and Cetraro, and one long hop of 50 miles between Cetraro and Vibo Valentia. Otherwise, for all intents and purposes, you can sail around the coast and choose where you will end up for the night. In the high season you will need to book ahead for marinas in popular areas around the Riviera, parts of Tuscany, the Pontine islands and Liparis, and marinas around Rome, but outside these popular areas you can usually turn up and find a berth. Yachts often miss out the mainland coast from Naples down to the Strait of Messina, which is a mistake as it has a lot to offer and is relatively uncrowded in the summer.

IT2 Corsica to the Italian west coast

Yachts can comfortably day-hop across from somewhere like Macinaggio or Bastia to Capraia and then on to Elba. Alternatively yachts cross from the Strait of Bonifacio to Ponza (around 180 miles) or to the Bay of Naples (240 miles). You need to watch for a weather window for the crossing to the Pontine islands or Bay of Naples as bad weather can move in surprisingly quickly and make it a very uncomfortable passage.

IT3 Southern Sardinia to Sicily or Tunisia

Yachts crossing to Sicily usually leave from somewhere like Cagliari or Villasimius and head for San Vito Lo Capo (around 160 miles) or Palermo (around 190 miles) on the north-west corner of Sicily. Yachts crossing to Tunisia will usually head for Ile de la Galite (around 100 miles) or Bizerte or Sidi Bou Said (around 125 miles). On both these passages, keep an eye on depressions coming in from the west as they can speed up through the area between Sardinia and Sicily and North Africa and it is hard to track their path.

IT4 Sicily and Malta

Yachts circulate either way around Sicily and can comfortably day-hop between harbours. The longest stretch without a good usable harbour is around 30 miles. Yachts normally cross from Ragusa or Porto Palo (both around 55 miles) to Valletta and although it is not far, it can be a bumpy passage across the Malta Channel with a significant amount of current. If crossing early or late in the season, pick your time with care as it can be very windy in the channel.

IT5 Sicily to the southern Adriatic and Greece

Yachts can opt for a direct passage across to Greece (Siracusa to Argostoli is around 280 miles) or coast along the toe and heel of Italy and then across to Othoni and Corfu. Cruising along the toe and heel means some long day passages with many of the hops between safe ports working out at 70–75 miles. Some care is also needed because you are on an exposed lee shore here if the weather brews up. From Santa Maria di Leuca, yachts head up into the Adriatic and usually cross to the Croatian side to

Savona on the Italian Riviera. Get into the inner basin and you are in the middle of town.

potter up among the islands, or to Corfu in Greece.

ADR1 Routes up the Adriatic

These involve either coasting up the east Italian coast or, more commonly, crossing to Croatia and coasting up through the islands to the northern Adriatic. When cruising up the Italian coast, there are numerous harbours to explore with distances of 30–40 miles between them up to Ravenna, after which harbours are more closely clustered together as you approach Venice. Some care is needed along this coast as much of it is fringed by shoal water; with strong onshore winds a heavy swell heaps up in the approaches to harbours. Around Venice and around to Slovenia there are numerous harbours within a short distance of each other. When sailing in

the Adriatic be aware that the *bora* can sweep down across the sea with little warning. The *sirocco* can also blow up here from the south in spring and autumn and can get up to force 7 or so.

Weather and seasons

Italy stretches for some 500 miles north and south; consequently the climate and winds vary dramatically depending on where you are. As a general rule it gets warmer the further south you go and in summer it can be stifling around Sicily and Calabria. In the north, the Riviera is on average a lot hotter than around Venice at the top of the Adriatic, where it is distinctly chilly in the winter.

For most of Italy, settled conditions begin around May and extend to September, although in the south you can be happily sailing by April and continue doing so until October. For the most part, sea breezes dominate the weather patterns in the summer although the local topography can change wind directions substantially. Around the Riviera the direction tends to be southerly becoming south-westerly as you proceed down the coast towards Naples and the Strait of Messina. There are numerous calm days and few gales in the summer. Depressions often pass across northern Italy and can give rise to strong winds in the Ligurian and northern Adriatic with the effects sometimes felt right down into the Tyrrhenian and southern Adriatic.

Around Sicily, westerlies predominate and around the toe and boot of Italy you will generally get southerlies. In the southern Adriatic the prevailing breeze is the *maistro* or *maestrale* which is fairly constantly from the north-west.

Formalities

As a member of the EU, Italy does not require other EU yachts to clear in or out. You may be asked for your papers and Customs and the Coastguard may make spot checks, usually around the southern Adriatic where there is a problem with Albanians crossing illegally into Italy.

Ashore

Like the French, the Italians have a passion for food and you will find good markets in most towns and large villages. Even quite small villages will have grocers, bakers and butchers with a wonderful selection of cheeses, hams, salamis, bread, pizzas and other produce. Large supermarkets are usually on the outskirts of town, though there will often be a medium-sized supermarket within a town.

Eating out in Italy is both a delight and not expensive if you choose wisely. Many restaurants have a *menu turistico*, a fixed price menu with two or three courses, and these can be excellent value. Italian cuisine rivals that of its neighbour France and you should not compare the food you get in Italy with some of the pallid lifeless versions you get in so-called Italian restaurants in the UK. Pizza and pasta are good examples of fare that can be exquisite in Italy compared to UK versions.

Yacht facilities

Most marinas will have a travel hoist, hardstanding and a range of services available and there are also boatyards independent of marinas. The most crowded areas are around the Riviera, Rome and Venice. Elsewhere you should not have too much trouble finding space to haul. Prices are generally cheaper around southern Italy.

Comparatively few boats winter afloat in Italy. What usually happens is that two or three cruisers get together and decide that they will winter somewhere afloat. San Remo, around Rome and Gaeta are popular. Other harbours that have been used include Savona, Genoa, Portoferraio, Cala Galera, Ischia, Salerno, Vibo Valentia, Alghero, Cagliari, Palermo and around Venice.

If you are hauling for the winter, a number of marina/yards have been popular in the past. For the most part there are few deals to be done and the price quoted will be close to the price paid. The following yards have been popular in recent years: Porto Maurizio, Santa Margherita Ligure, Lavagna, Le Grazie, Edilnautica Marina (Elba), Marina di Carrara, Viareggio, Porto San Stefano, Fiumare Grande, Base Nautica Flavio Gioia, Salerno, Olbia, Trapani, Sibaris and around Trieste.

Marine reserves

Italy has by far the most comprehensive network of marine reserves in the Mediterranean: there are 25 dotted around its coasts and islands. These nature and marine reserves are intended to protect the natural biodiversity in areas of special interest, and to encourage the widening of knowledge of these sensitive ecosystems. The reserves protect geological and biological environments, birds, fish and mammals, as well as vegetation. One example is the laying of moorings and restricting of anchoring to protect *Posidonia Oceanica*, seagrass

Amalfi harbour on the Sorrento Peninsula.

beds which are an important breeding area for certain fish.

There are three types of restricted zones. The interpretation below is my paraphrasing of the legalese in the Italian original and contains the gist of the regulations.

Zone A Riserva Integrale

- It is prohibited to navigate or anchor, fish, pollute in any way including black or grey water, or to remove any plant, mineral or animal life in the designated area.
- Bathing is restricted to designated areas.

Zone B Riserva Generale

- It is prohibited to carry out any form of fishing.
- Navigation and mooring are permitted, although there may be specific restrictions at any one reserve.

Zone C Riserva Parziale

- Commercial fishing is prohibited.
- Sport fishing may be limited in some areas.

New and existing national parks and marine reserves change their status on a regular basis and you are strongly advised to consult the respective authority prior to arrival.

Yachts wishing to visit La Maddalena Archipelago must obtain a yacht permit, available at La Maddalena or Palau. Permits may be purchased on a daily, fortnightly or monthly rate.

For information and links to all the National Parks and Marine Reserves see www.parks.it

Airports

In recent years, the number of airports served by low cost airlines has multiplied and Italy now has a wide range of flights available. The following airports are used by low cost airlines: Genoa, Milan, Pisa, Rome, Naples, Lamezia (Calabria), Alghero, Cagliari, Sardinia, Trapani, Palermo (Sicily), Pescara, Ancona, Venice and Trieste. Internal flights in Italy are good value and it's worth looking at flying to a main hub like Rome and getting a flight from there.

Shoestring cruising

In general, marinas are more expensive in the north and get cheaper as you go south. There are always exceptions and it is important to check the price band of a marina before assuming it will be reasonable because you are in southern Italy. Around the Bay of Naples and Sicily, for example, there are some expensive marinas scattered in among the less expensive ones. High season charges are from around 1 July through to mid-September. An increasing number of marinas are now starting high season prices earlier, often in May, and extending high season to October. Some are also introducing a mid-season price which runs from April through to May or June and from September to November. In Italy, high season charges, aiming to capture all the Continental holidaymakers in July and August, can be two or even three times the low season charge, so it makes sense to plan ahead carefully; if possible avoid cruising in July and August, when some areas will be impossibly crowded.

If you are going from north to south then the more expensive areas are around the Italian Riviera, Rome and the Bay of Naples, the northern end of Sardinia,

and near Venice. You can, for example, cruise economically in the high season by anchoring around the Tuscan islands and along the coast of Tuscany, stepping carefully down the coast past Rome and the Bay of Naples using cheaper harbours and some anchorages, then along the coast between Naples and the Strait of Messina, around the bottom of Italy and up to the area near Ravenna where, with care and a little research, you can find cheaper harbours; around Venice you can anchor or choose your marinas with care. Over in Sardinia, most marinas have reasonable charges apart from the north coast; and there are enough useful anchorages to avoid expensive marinas. Around Sicily, prices are reasonable although an increasing number of the marinas there are charging at charge band 5 and above in the high season. Fortunately there are anchorages you can use around the southern side of Sicily; the northern side has fewer anchorages.

In the high season you need to be careful of places that appear simple: maybe just a rough wooden catwalk with some laid moorings – these can charge very high prices. Ormegiatori lease a part of a quay or the right to build a catwalk and charge yachts for the service. In some places this can be a modest charge, but it can be out of all proportion to the services offered. Take advice from other cruisers and see what charge band was operating last time.

Although there are not a lot of good anchorages, with the exception of northern Sardinia, it is surprising how much of the Italian coast you can visit and find anchorages that, if not always comfortable, are tenable in settled weather. Like France, I've covered the coast of Italy using a mix of anchorages and marinas and while some of the anchorages may have been uncomfortable at times, at least there was usually a marina nearby if the weather deteriorated. The only drawback is that the Coastguard may become curious about your solitary presence in an anchorage when everyone else is in harbour.

Reading
Italian Waters Pilot, Rod Heikell, Imray.
Pagine Azzure, annual almanac in Italian.
Adriatic Pilot, T & D Thompson, Imray.
Imray Mediterranean Almanac, edited by Rod Heikell, Imray.

MALTA

Malta principally consists of two small islands between Sicily and Tunisia. It has long been used as a naval base and it is a place to winter or visit for spares and repairs and to stock up on provisions.

Cruising area
The two islands of Malta and Gozo have few natural anchorages and only a handful of harbours. Most yachts cross to Sicily or Tunisia to go cruising. The route to Tunisia usually involves a hop across to Lampedusa (or sometimes Pantelleria) and then on to somewhere like El Kantaoui or Monastir in the Gulf of Hammamet.

Weather and seasons
Malta has a hot summer and mild winter making it an ideal base for over-wintering. Winds in the summer are mostly from the west. In the winter, severe gales can blow over the islands from the west or east with the *gregale* being especially bothersome as it tends to set up a surge in Marsamxett.

Formalities
All yachts must clear into Malta at either Grand Harbour or at Mgarr on Gozo. Call up on VHF Ch16 or 12 when 10 miles off Malta.

Ashore
Malta is a good place to stock up on some basic provisions, though not fresh fruit and vegetables. There is a supermarket near Msida Marina and others in Gzira. There are good restaurants with a quasi-English/ international cuisine and enough bars to keep most people happy.

Yacht facilities
There are five marinas. Grand Harbour marina and Portomaso are fairly up-market, while Msida Marina and Manoel Island costs less and are better situated than the other two. Mgarr on the southern end of Gozo makes up the quintet. There are a number of new small marinas around Valetta and on Gozo, but they are generally open only in the high season. There are several boatyards and a wide range of boat facilities including good chandlers and agents for marine gear.

Airports
Daily flights to the UK from Malta.

Reading
Italian Waters Pilot, Rod Heikell, Imray. (It includes Malta.)

Dwerja anchorage on Gozo.

SLOVENIA, CROATIA, MONTENEGRO AND ALBANIA

When the former Yugoslavia disintegrated, Croatia inherited most of the coast and islands. Slovenia is sandwiched between Croatia and Italy with a couple of marinas on its short coastline; at the southern end, Bosnia-Herzegovina gets a small bite of the coast while Montenegro gets a chunk between Dubrovnik and Albania. Now that things are quiet, the area has again become popular with yachtsmen and many of the marinas are now crowded with yachts based permanently or semi-permanently here. After all, this wonderful Mediterranean playground is only a short drive from southern Germany, Austria and northern Italy.

The archipelago of islands running down the coast, combined with a much indented coastline, provides a superb sailing area. There are sufficient marinas and harbours and plenty of well-sheltered anchorages to make up a large and varied cruising area. The scenery is spectacular, with high mountains bordering many shores and some wonderful old towns and villages scattered around the coast.

Montenegro gained independence from Serbia in 2006 and, along with Croatia, is seeking EU membership. Near the southern border, Bar has Montenegro's first marina, and more have opened in the Gulf of Kotor, which offers several harbours and an interesting cruising area.

The Albanian coast is relatively straight and is little cruised by yachts. Harbours have few facilities, but there is one 'marina' in Vlore near the border with Greece. Albania has seen some piracy incidents in the past, but with

147

increased political stability the tourist industry is beginning to develop, and yachts are slowly returning. Italian and Greek naval vessels patrol here, looking for boats carrying drugs or *clandestinis* (stowaways) and security in the towns and harbours is generally good.

Cruising routes

ADR1

Most yachts entering the Adriatic choose to cross into Croatia rather than sail up the comparatively straight east coast of Italy. In the southern Adriatic, the prevailing north-north-westerly day breeze means that a direct route will mean beating up past Albania and Montenegro to get to Dubrovnik. Many yachts choose to cling to the Italian coast or cross from Greece across to Italy before crossing to Korčula from somewhere like Manfredonia or the Isole Tremiti. Yachts that leave from harbours further south like Bari or Brindisi will often head for Dubrovnik and depart in the late evening when the prevailing wind dies down, motoring through the night to get as many miles in as possible before the wind gets up again mid-morning. From Isole Tremiti it is around 80 miles to Korčula and from Brindisi around 135 miles to Dubrovnik.

Once you are in Croatia, it is possible to day-hop from one end to the other and still choose where you will stop for the night.

Weather and seasons

The Adriatic is nearly 500 miles long in roughly a NW–SE direction, so it is not surprising that there are significant differences between weather at the top and bottom. Weather at the top is more akin to Continental weather, with some rain in the summer and chilly winds in the spring and autumn. In the south, the weather is more Mediterranean with a hotter summer and a more clement spring and autumn.

The prevailing wind in the Adriatic is the *maestral* blowing from north-west at the bottom of the Adriatic to west in the middle and south-west at the top. It is a sea breeze so normally gets up around midday and blows through until early evening. It is much altered by the high land and channels between the islands so its direction here is more variable. In the spring and sometimes in the summer a *jugo* (*sirocco*) will blow up the Adriatic, reaching force 6 or so. In the winter, spring and autumn, the *bora* can blow down from the north-east with great violence and has been known to get up to force 10 or more. It is usually strongest in the Velebit Channel and the Gulf of Trieste, but there are other known bad *bora* corridors including Kvarner, Šibenik, Split, Makarska, Pelješac and Dubrovnik. Sometimes in the summer, a mild version of the *bora*, the *burino*, will blow down from the north-east at around force 5–6.

Formalities

All yachts entering Croatia must go to a port of entry within 24 hours to present the yacht's papers and obtain a sailing permit. A permit, along with an adhesive sticker for your boat, is valid for one year and entitles you to cruise all Croatian waters including leaving and re-entering Croatia. Whether you are cruising for

Squeezing onto the quay in Croatia.

a week or a year, the permit costs the same: in 2011 it cost around €300 for a 12-metre yacht. In addition you need to pay a tourist tax or 'sojourn' fee depending on your length of stay. For a 12-metre yacht getting a 90 day 'sojourn' permit the cost in 2011 was around €85. Along with the permit you will be given details on the rules and regulations for cruising Croatia and on weather forecasts and the like.

Croatian ports of entry: Dubrovnik, Korčula, Metković, Ploče, Split, Šibenik, Zadar, Maslenica, Senj, Mali Losinj, Rijeka, Rasa-Brsica, Pula, Rovinj, Poreč, Umag. Summer only: Ubli, Vis, Hvar, Ravni Zakan, Primosten, Soline, Sali, Novigrad.

Slovenia and Montenegro have separate entry formalities which also involve clearing and paying a cruising fee. Slovenian ports of entry: Koper, Piran. Montenegro ports of entry: Bar, Budva, Herceg Novi, Kotor.

In Albania, port dues must be paid in cash and it is necessary to clear in and out of each port, so if stopping in several ports it is relatively expensive.

Ashore

Croatia has not enjoyed a good reputation for the quality of its natural ingredients or the way they are put together in the national cruisine. I remember some appalling stews and gruel from so-called restaurants in the days of the former Yugoslavia. Happily, nowadays, the choice of provisions available and the fare in most restaurants is much improved.

In most towns and larger villages you can buy a wide range of provisions including many imported goods from the EU and particularly nearby Italy. In most places there will be a bakery with a range of bread and grocer's and butcher's shops. Some of the Croatian produce, such as hams and salamis, are good along with soft white cheeses. On some of the islands it can be more difficult to find everything so you should stock up when possible in larger towns.

Restaurant meals mostly consist of grilled or barbecued meat or fish with the ubiquitous chips but are generally OK. A lot of quasi-Italian restaurants offering pasta and pizza have also appeared. Look for restaurants serving some of the stews and stuffed dishes closer to the traditional local cuisine as these are worth trying.

Yacht facilities

Croatia has about 45 marinas of which the majority (22) are run by ACI (Adriatic Croatia International Club). Some of these marinas are closed in the winter. Most of the marinas that are open throughout the year will have a travel hoist, hardstanding and a range of services available; there are also a few boatyards independent of marinas. In recent years, demand on hauling and storage for the winter has been high and you should endeavour to book ahead in popular areas.

Yachts wintering afloat congregate at the southern end of the Adriatic for the simple reason that it can get very cold in the winter towards the north. The popularity of Croatia means that long-term spaces for the winter are much in demand and you should book ahead for storage ashore.

Popular marinas for those wintering afloat include: Dubrovnik, Korčula, Split and Zadar. Bar Marina in Montenegro is also building a reputation for competitively priced winter storage.

Airports

Low cost airlines now fly to Ljubliana, Split, Zadar, Pula and Dubrovnik. There are charter flights to Dubrovnik, Split, Brac, Zadar and Pula in the summer.

Shoestring cruising

Marina charges in Croatia vary from moderate to high, so it is worth checking ahead to see what the price band is. Most municipal harbours make a charge which is usually reasonable, depending on the facilities available. It also depends on the amount of quay-space you occupy, so going alongside costs more than stern- or bows-to berthing. The large number of anchorages around the mainland coast and islands mean that you can easily potter up through Croatia and rarely visit a marina or harbour once you have paid your annual cruising permit fee and the 'sojourn' fee for your length of stay. In some places the authorities charge for anchoring, the amount varying according to the services offered (whether on a laid mooring, for refuse collection, etc). In recent years moorings in some areas and even the charge for anchoring has increased steeply and overnight charges of up to €50 have been reported. Anyone collecting fees must give an official receipt.

Reading

Adriatic Pilot, T & D Thompson, Imray.
Navigational Guide to the Adriatic-Croatian Coast, Leksikografski Zavod, Croatian Hydrographic Office publication.
777 Harbours & Anchorages – Croatia, Slovenia & Montenegro Karl & Anna Bestrandig & Rod Bailey, Magnamare.
Imray Mediterranean Almanac, edited by Rod Heikell, Imray.

GREECE

The much indented coastline and the large number of islands make Greece the largest cruising ground in the Mediterranean and it has been a popular sailing area for some time. Most of the coast is mountainous, with depths dropping off quickly, and many of the islands are, in fact, the peaks of mountains standing on a plain which was flooded millions of years ago. The sea area is broken up into two major seas, the Ionian on the western side and the Aegean between the Peloponnese and Turkey. These two seas are sub-divided into a number of smaller named seas: Kithera, Cretan, Kos-Rhodos, Samos and Thasos. The coast is usually divided up as follows:

Northern Ionian from Corfu down to Zakinthos and adjacent coast A superb sailing area and consequently one of the most popular areas in Greece.

Southern Ionian This comprises the western and southern Peloponnese and a few off-lying islands. Infrequently visited by yachts.

Gulf of Patras and Gulf of Corinth The two gulfs separating the Peloponnese from mainland Greece. Mostly used as a route between the Ionian and Aegean though it is an excellent cruising area in its own right.

Saronic and eastern Peloponnese This comprises the Attic coast around Athens and the eastern Peloponnese and off-lying islands. Parts are crowded in the summer with boats based in the marinas around Athens.

Cyclades These central Aegean islands are scattered between the Peloponnese and the Dodecanese. Some are popular in the summer but others are little visited. All the Cyclades are swept by the *meltemi* in the summer.

Evia and northern Sporades While the

The chora on Astipalaia.

Simi in the Dodecanese. There are lots of wonderful harbours like this around the islands and mainland coast.

Cruising routes

GR1 Ionian to the Aegean

Yachts can either sail around the Peloponnese or cut through the Gulfs of Patras and Corinth and the Corinth Canal. Both routes have favourable winds when going east and generally contrary winds going west. There are plenty of harbours and anchorages to choose from. If you are headed for Athens then the Corinth Canal route makes sense. If you are headed for the Argolic Gulf and islands like Spetsai and Poros, there is not a lot to choose between the two routes and if headed for anywhere between Milos and Crete then the route around the Peloponnese makes more sense.

GR2 Aegean routes

Summer routes through the Aegean are determined by the *meltemi*. Generally it blows from June to September from the north-east through north to north-west, describing an arc from the Dardenelles through the central Aegean to Rhodes. While it is possible to beat up to the northern Aegean against the *meltemi*, the sensible option is go north before the *meltemi* sets in and then go south in the summer when it is blowing. If you need to go north late in the season, plan to do so after the *meltemi* has finished. Likewise, leaving from Turkey or the Dodecanese to go west will mean beating against it so yachts should leave before or after the *meltemi* season.

With so many harbours and anchorages scattered around and across the Aegean there are no really defined routes and it is up to you where you stop en route.

northern Sporades are popular, Evia and the adjacent mainland coast are less so.
Northern Greece This stretch of mainland coast between Thessaloniki and Turkey is popular around the Khalkidhiki, but otherwise most of it is little visited.
Eastern Sporades This chain of islands from Limnos to Samos is infrequently visited although it makes a wonderful cruising area.
Dodecanese. Patmos to Rhodes A superb, if windy, cruising area popular in the summer.
Crete A few harbours in Crete are popular, but in general it is little visited.

Port Atheni on Meganisi in the Ionian.

Weather and seasons

Greece conforms pretty much to the ideal of a Mediterranean climate with hot dry summers and cool wet winters. This means that it has a long cruising season and is a popular place to overwinter.

In the summer, the prevailing winds in the Ionian and the Aegean are northerlies. In the Ionian the *maistro* is the prevailing wind blowing from the north-west to north-north-west in the southern Peloponnese. It is a sea breeze that gets up around midday and dies down in the evening. In the Aegean, the *meltemi* is the prevailing summer wind blowing from the north-east in the north through north in the central region to north-west in the south-east. At times the meltemi can blow strongly, often F6–7 or more. When northerlies are not blowing there can be a sea breeze and its concomitant effect on other prevailing winds whereby the sea breeze can augment or decrease wind from another direction.

In the spring or autumn care is needed when depressions pass across or near the area, often bringing southerlies.

Formalities

Greece is a member of the EU though it has introduced its own 'traffic document' for all yachts. All yachts entering Greece should fly the Greek courtesy ensign and should proceed to a port of entry. The authorities should be visited in the following order: PASSPORT CONTROL (IMMIGRATION) – HEALTH – CUSTOMS – PORT POLICE. All yachts entering from countries outside the EU should fly a Q flag, and will need to complete full immigration and customs clearance.

Yachts entering Greece from within the EU are not required to clear customs, but non-EU registered yachts need to obtain a Transit Log from customs officials. Non-EU passport holders will first need to complete immigration formalities and obtain visas if necessary.

The Transit Log is a customs record for non-EU yachts visiting the EU. It is valid for six months, and must be surrendered when the yacht leaves Greece. Most non-EU registered yachts are subject to a reciprocal tax of €15 per metre, every three months, levied at the end of the period.

All yachts over 10m LOA must purchase a traffic document (DEKPA) from the Port Police. The DEKPA is valid for fifty ports of call, and should be presented to Port Police to stamp on entering and leaving each port, when harbour dues will also be collected. In practice the DEKPA is not inspected regularly, though you should endeavour to get a few stamps through the year. It may be reused even after the yacht has left and re-entered Greece. The cost of the DEKPA is €30.

Ashore

In most places you will have few problems getting basic provisions at mini-markets. In recent years large supermarkets like Carrefour, Dia and Lidl have opened with shelves stacked with most of the things you can buy throughout Europe. Often these are on the outskirts of a town so you will need a car or a bicycle to get there. Smaller shops in town will stock most things you need and you would be surprised at what can be packed into a relatively small space. In recent years, the choice of imported goods has increased and some larger manufacturers distribute things like vacuum-packed cheeses, sausages and bacon. Entry to the EU has meant that fruit and vegetables are no longer

as seasonal as in the past although the imported produce is not as tasty as the locally grown fruit and vegetables.

Eating out in Greece has rarely been a gourmet experience although some tavernas are beginning to edge away from the usual bland chips-with-something-grilled. The location of many of the tavernas makes up for the lack of attention to food, so maybe just settle for a Greek salad and a charcoal-grilled pork chop and enjoy the sunset on that wine dark sea. Increasingly, you will find places that care about food, so you'll get tasty fare *and* the idyllic view.

Yacht facilities

Some of the marinas in Greece have a yard and hauling services as part of the deal, but most boatyards are independent affairs. Around Greece there is a mix of yards hauling by travel hoist, hydraulic trailer, using a sledge and runners or a mobile crane with strops. You should not be put off by yards using a sledge and runners or a hydraulic trailer as these methods are as safe as a travel hoist.

Greece has a good climate for wintering aboard although it still gets chilly in the winter. A number of places are popular, although allegiances change and the numbers wintering afloat fluctuate. The following places have been used in the past: Corfu (Gouvia), Preveza, Levkas and Nidri, Kalamata Marina, Trizonia, Zea marina, Aigina, Poros, Porto Kheli, Lakki (Leros), Rhodes, Ayios Nikolaos (Crete) and Khania.

If you are hauling for the winter, a number of Greek marinas and yards have been popular in the past few years. You can do a bit of haggling over price, but in general the price quoted will be what you pay. In some of the yards, outside workers are not allowed to work on boats so check out the situation if you intend to use outside contractors. The following yards are worth investigating: Gouvia, Aktion (Preveza), Levkás, Nidri, Katakolon, Salamis, Ambelakia, Aigina, Poros, Porto Kheli, Koiladhia, Siros, Olympic Marine, Volos, Vathoudhi, Partheni (Leros) and Kos Marina.

Airports

EasyJet flies to Athens, Corfu, Thessaloniki, Mikonos, Iraklion (Crete) and Rhodes and in the summer there are charter flights to Corfu, Preveza, Cephalonia, Zakinthos, Kalamata, Athens, Mikonos, Paros, Thira, Skiathos, Thessaloniki, Samos, Kos, Rhodes and Iraklion. If you are flying to Athens there are internal flights all over Greece although these are often heavily booked up. In the future it is likely there will be more low cost airlines flying to Greek airports.

Shoestring cruising

Greece has so many anchorages scattered around the coast and islands that you could, conceivably, never have to go into a harbour. After you have paid for your cruising permit you are free to anchor anywhere. Marinas in Greece are generally around charge band 3. In most harbours the cost for a 12-metre yacht in 2010 was a tad under €10 a night, that is if the port police bother to charge you.

Not surprisingly Greece attracts a large number of shoestring cruising yachts, though in some harbours and anchorages,

where some yachts have become little more than static houseboats, the locals understandably get upset at the floating rubbish heap moored in their backyard and yachts have been moved along.

Reading

Greek Waters Pilot, Rod Heikell, Imray.
Ionian, Rod Heikell, Imray. Covers the northern Ionian.
West Aegean, Rod Heikell, Imray. Covers the Attic coast, eastern Peloponnese and western Cyclades.
East Aegean, Rod Heikell, Imray. Covers the Dodecanese and adjacent Turkish coast.
Imray Mediterranean Almanac, edited by Rod Heikell, Imray.

TURKEY

Turkey has a long coast that is mostly bordered by high mountains that drop sheer into the sea. There are few off-lying islands, though parts of the coast are much indented with deep gulfs and it is these areas that are the popular cruising grounds. Four seas border the Turkish coast:

Black Sea This is a fairly straight coast with spectacular mountains rising steeply from the sea. It has few natural harbours and bays and most of the shelter is provided by man-made harbours. It is little cruised by yachts.
Marmara Sea This sea is closed off at the northern end by the Bosphorus and at the southern end by the Dardanelles. Usually used as a route from Istanbul down to the Aegean, it makes up an interesting

Anchored under Bodrum Castle in the Gulf of Gokova.

mini-cruising area in its own right.
Aegean The Turkish coast is bordered
by the Aegean from just above the
Dardanelles down to around Rhodes.
Several large gulfs bite back into the coast
and it makes a popular cruising area,
particularly south of Kuşadaşi.
South-east Mediterranean Apart from
the Gulf of Fethiye and around Kekova,
this is a fairly straight coastline. From
Antalya there are few natural harbours
and the coast is little cruised.

Cruising routes

TUR1 The Aegean coast and around to Antalya

Along this coast there are numerous
harbours and anchorages within short
distances so that yachts on passage can
choose where they bring up for the night.
If heading north it is best to do so very
early or late in the season so you are not
constantly bashing into headwinds when
the *meltemi* is blowing.

TUR2 The Mediterranean coast and passage to Cyprus

Yachts can cruise around the Med coast
with just one or two legs of 40–50 miles
where you will need to leave early in the
morning to get to the next harbour by
dusk. Some care is needed along parts
of the coast as the prevailing sea breeze
blows obliquely onto the land, making it
a lee shore.

Yachts en route to Cyprus often leave
from somewhere like Kas or Finike for
Paphos (150 miles) or Limassol (200
miles) which usually involves just one

Kale Kay and restaurant pontoons in Kekova in eastern Turkey.

night out. After you clear the Turkish coast, until you get to 10–20 miles off Cyprus, there will often be no wind or light breezes for much of the night if there are no depressions around. Yachts en route to northern Cyprus will often coast around to Alanya or Taşucu and then cross to Kyrenia.

TUR3 Sea of Marmara and Black Sea
Passage up the Dardanelles and Sea of Marmara is directly against the prevailing *meltemi* and against the current (which can be considerable in places), so it usually involves lots of stops in harbours and anchorages. Passage back down the Sea of Marmara is with the prevailing wind and current. Passages in the Black Sea are usually along the Turkish Black Sea coast, where there are numerous harbours and anchorages, or up to Bulgaria and Romania.

Weather and seasons
The climate in Turkey varies considerably from north to south-east. In the north above Ayvalik, the season is shorter compared to further south around Kuşadasi and Bodrum. Istanbul can be very cold, wet and foggy in the winter. South from Kuşadasi, the climate is typically Mediterranean with hot dry summers and cool wet winters. This means it has a long cruising season and is a popular place to overwinter. From Antalya east it can be very hot and humid in the summer and winters are correspondingly milder.

The *meltemi* blows down the Turkish Aegean coast from north to north-east, curving around to the west and south-west after Rhodes. In the north, the *meltemi* tends to blow out of the gulfs, while in the south it tends to blow mostly into the gulfs. East from Kekova, the prevailing wind is a sea breeze that normally sets in around midday and can blow up to force 5–6 at times from the south to south-west or south-east depending on the orientation of the coast and local topography. At night and in the morning, there can be a fairly strong land breeze blowing off the coast until the sea breeze sets in.

Formalities

All yachts must go first to a port of entry and clear in. A transit log will be issued which is valid for one year, one continuous visit, or until the yacht is laid-up – whichever happens first. When leaving Turkey with the yacht you must surrender the transit log, even if you intend to return to Turkey *at any time*. The transit log cost €30 in 2011. You will usually need to employ an agent to do the paperwork, which will cost around €50. A 3-month visa is automatically given on entry and if you want to stay longer you can leave the yacht in Turkey and clear in and out (usually by ferry to Greece) to obtain another 3-month visa. The exception is if you have an annual (or longer) contract in a marina, when you can obtain a visa for a year (or longer depending on the length of the contract).

Ports of entry: Istanbul, Bandırma, Canakkale, Ayvalık, Dikili, Izmir, Cesme, Kuşadası, Güllük, Bodrum, Datca, Marmaris, Fethiye, Kaş, Finike, Kemer, Antalya, Alanya, Anamur, Bozyazi, Taşucu, Mersin, Iskenderun.

Ashore

In most places there will be, at the very least, a mini-market where all of the basics can be found. In larger towns there will be a wider choice of products and often a large supermarket on the outskirts of town where everything can be found. There will often be a weekly market (often on a Friday) where the farmers come to town with some of the best fruit and vegetables to be found in the Mediterranean, as well as other local produce including dried fruit and nuts, cheeses, herbs and spices and honey.

Turkish cuisine is excellent and as renowned in the east as French cuisine is in the west. The food is varied and inexpensive and the service good. Even in quite small coves you will find rustic huts offering food during the summer. In towns and resorts you will be spoilt for choice with everything from soups, a wide range of *mezes*, stews and oven dishes, grilled meat and fish, *pides* (Turkish pizzas), all with salad and, in this age of tourism, the ubiquitous chips.

Yacht facilities

Most of the marinas in Turkey will have a travel hoist and a hardstanding area with some yacht repair facilities. There are also independent yards which use a travel hoist or a sledge and runners. Most yacht repairs and even major work like osmosis treatment and painting GRP hulls, electrical and electronic work, wood and engineering work can be carried out. As always, it pays to check just who is carrying out the work as the quality and attention to detail varies from place to place.

Turkey has a good climate for wintering aboard and reasonable winter contract prices; the relatively cheap cost of living means that many of the marinas are popular for live-aboards. Allegiances vary, but the following places have been used in the past: Kuşadası, Bodrum, Marti Marina (Orhaniye), Marmaris, Gocek, Finike, Kemer and Antalya.

If you are hauling for the winter, a number of marina/yards have been popular places in the past. There is not a lot of haggling to be done over prices which are pretty much fixed. As in Greece, check with the yards to see if outside workers are permitted to work on your boat. The following yards have been popular: Ayvalık, Kuşadası, Yalikavak, Turgutreis, Bodrum and Icmeler, Marti Marina, Marmaris, Gocek, Finike, Kemer and Antalya.

Airports

There are regular scheduled flights to Turkey and charter flights in the summer. EasyJet flies to Istanbul, Izmir, Bodrum and Dalaman. Pegasus, a Turkish low-cost airline, also flies to European destinations. Charter airlines fly to Istanbul, Izmir, Bodrum, Dalaman and Antalya. You can also fly to Greece and get a ferry across, although a Turkish stamp in your passport may invalidate a return flight.

Shoestring cruising

Marinas in Turkey have become more expensive of late and for a 12-metre yacht some are now charge band 4 or 5. Most marinas don't have a low season charge and the daily cost is the same summer and winter. There are still marinas around at charge band 2-3 so do some research

to find out what costs are. Annual contracts at most Turkish marinas are still competitive. One of the 'problems' with Turkish marinas is that they are nearly all 5 star affairs with well appointed facilities that would not disgrace a 5 star hotel. There are not too many 2 or 3 star marinas around. Many municipal harbours charge at around charge band 2/3. Along the coast and in the gulfs there are a large number of anchorages, and for most of the Aegean coast and around to Antalya you can pretty much get by without going into a harbour. Turkey still attracts its fair share of shoestring cruisers and has a significant number of live-aboards spending the winter here.

Reading

Turkish Waters and Cyprus Pilot, Rod Heikell, Imray.

East Aegean, Rod Heikell, Imray. Covers the Dodecanese and adjacent Turkish coast.

Imray Mediterranean Almanac, edited by Rod Heikell, Imray.

Cruise the Black Sea, Doreen and Archie Annan, RCC.

CYPRUS

The island of Cyprus lies tucked up between Turkey and the Levant. It has been divided into northern and southern Cyprus since the Turkish invasion in 1974. Southern Cyprus entered the EU in 2004.

Cruising area

The large island has few natural anchorages and a handful of harbours. Most yachts cross to Turkey or Greece to cruise.

Dislice Adasi in the Gulf of Hisaronu. (Photo Kadir Kir.)

Weather and seasons

Cyprus has a hot summer and mild winter making it an ideal base for over-wintering. Winds in the summer are mostly a sea breeze from the west. In the winter, gales are mostly from depressions passing south of the island.

Formalities

Yachts headed for southern Cyprus should clear in at Paphos, Limassol or Larnaca. The relevant authorities are located nearby or in Larnaca within the marina. Yachts heading for northern Cyprus should clear in at Girne (Kyrenia).

Ashore

Cyprus is a good place to stock up on basic provisions including many English favourites like marmite and tea. There are good supermarkets at Larnaca and it is a logical place for provisioning if headed towards the Red Sea. There are good restaurants with a quasi-English/international cuisine and some good *meze* restaurants tucked away in the back streets.

Yacht facilities

Cyprus is a popular spot to overwinter and you need to book well ahead to get a place at Larnaca. Most yacht spares can be found here and there is a good yard in the marina. Northern Cyprus now has the recently completed Karpaz Gate Marina and another is nearly complete.

Reading

Turkish Waters and Cyprus Pilot, Rod Heikell, Imray.
Imray Mediterranean Almanac, edited by Rod Heikell, Imray.

SYRIA, LEBANON, ISRAEL, EGYPT AND LIBYA

Few yachts cruise these coasts with the exception of the Eastern Mediterranean Yacht Rally, where yachts cruise in company around this area. Some yachts will head off on their own for Syria, Lebanon and Israel, but in general these coasts are little cruised. Yachts headed for Egypt will usually be going to Port Said to transit the Suez Canal and on down into the Red Sea.

Syria

Note: The continuing conflict in Syria at the time of writing means that yachts should avoid entering Syrian territorial waters until the FCO advises otherwise.

Yachts normally head for Lattakia where you can clear in and obtain a shore pass. For travel inland you will need a visa. Apart from Lattakia there are harbours at Banias, Ṭarṭoūs and Ile de Rouad which can be used.

Lebanon

Yachts may not enter Lebanese waters if coming from Israel. Yachts should make for Jounie Marina, Beirut Marina or Marina Joseph Koury as these are really the only three harbours equipped to deal with yachts. Call up on VHF Ch11, 16 when 12 miles out to get instructions and then proceed, monitoring the VHF.

Israel

Yachts must call the Israeli Navy when 25 miles out on Ch16 to advise of arrival off the coast. It is imperative that you follow this procedure and all subsequent instructions. You may be shadowed by a patrol boat into Israeli waters and should comply with all their requests. Yachts must proceed to a port of entry at Haifa, Tel Aviv, Ashdod or Ashkelon where you will be cleared in.

Israel has some yachting infrastructure and some repairs and spares can be found here.

Egypt

Note: After the '18 day revolution' in Egypt in early 2011 that ousted Mubarrak things seem to have settled

Local lateen rigged boat in the Suez Canal.

down and tourists are slowly returning to the country. It would still pay to keep an eye on developments here.

Most yachts will be heading for Port Said to transit the Suez Canal. You should call up on VHF Ch16 to advise the port authorities of your arrival. You will almost certainly be contacted by radio and/or bumboat by agents touting for your business. If possible arrange an agent in advance. At Port Said you should proceed to the Port Fouad Yacht Club and tie up there.

In the winter when much of the Mediterranean braces itself for chillier weather and cold Slavic winds bringing ice and snow, Egypt's Red Sea coast settles down to more convivial temperatures in the twenties. As winter comes to the Mediterranean some yachts are avoiding the cold by taking the snowbird trail to Egypt. A short voyage down to the Port Said and a transit through the Suez Canal leads to the warm waters of the Red Sea. Once through the canal, though there is plenty to detain a yacht in Ismalia and Port Suez, it is possible to daysail down to Hurgadha and take a winter berth in either Hurgadha Marina or Abu Tig Marina nearby. These marinas do some good winter deals though repair facilities are few and far between so take whatever spares you might need.

Libya

Note: At the time of writing the situation in Libya is confused, with the National Transitional Council in charge until elections can be arranged.

A visa obtained in advance is necessary for a visit to Libya. Visas are usually only issued to foreigners working in Libya although there are signs that Libya is opening up and access will be easier in the future.

Further reading
Imray Mediterranean Almanac, edited by Rod Heikell, Imray.

TUNISIA

Note: After the 'Jasmine revolution' in Tunisia that ousted Ben Ali in early 2011 things seem to have settled down. It would still pay to keep an eye on things here if you are planning to go.

Sandwiched in between the relatively straight coastlines of Libya and Algeria,

Tunisia offers the best cruising area on the North African coast. It can be divided up into the north coast between Tabarka and Cape Bon and the east coast between Kelibia to the Libyan border. The east coast is the preferred cruising area for most yachts with a number of marinas and fishing harbours and anchorages.

Cruising routes

TUN1 Tunisia east coast
This coast is relatively low-lying with extensive shallows extending out in places. There are sufficient harbours to make day-hops straightforward. The relatively shallow waters mean that there can be significant tidal streams. Yachts heading for Malta will usually leave from somewhere like Monastir or El Kantaoui and make for Pantellaria or Lampedusa before proceeding to Malta and Sicily.

TUN2 Tunisia north coast
Around the north coast there are sufficient harbours and anchorages to day-hop. Yachts will often leave from anywhere between Kelibia and Sidi Bou Said for the western end of Sicily or for Sardinia. Care is needed to pick a suitable weather window for this passage as strong winds can kick up considerable seas in the Sicilian Strait.

Weather and seasons
Tunisia has hot dry summers and mild winters. Some areas can get a surprising amount of rain in winter though most falls in the north and little in the far south.

The prevailing wind in the summer is a sea breeze getting up around midday and blowing through to early evening.

On the northern coast it blows from the north-west. On the east coast it blows from the east although there is a daily variation with it starting in the north-east and moving through east to south-east in the evening. It can get up to force 5–6 at times. At night there can be a light land breeze blowing off the coast.

Formalities

On arrival at an entry port you need to obtain a triptique which must be surrendered when you leave Tunisia. The triptique is for 3 months, renewable for another 3 months; for the remaining 6 months, a yacht can be put under Customs seal (*plombage*), ashore or afloat.

Ashore

Most provisions can be found in villages and towns although you will have to adapt to local brands. In the larger towns and cities there are French Monoprix and other supermarkets with a wide range of goods. Most towns have local markets where you will find good fruit and vegetables and other local produce.

Eating out varies from French-influenced restaurants in the cities and large towns to local establishments in villages. The cuisine is typically North African with some fairly spicy *couscous* and *tajine* dishes. Costs are relatively cheap.

Yacht facilities

There are travel hoists at Sidi Bou Said, El Kantaoui and Monastir. There are also travel hoists and yards with a sledge and runners in some fishing harbours. Yacht repair facilities are not well developed but basic engineering work can be carried out.

Tunisia has a good climate for wintering aboard and reasonable winter contract prices, and the relatively cheap cost of living mean that many of the marinas are popular for live-aboards. Most live-aboards winter in one of the marinas at El Kantaoui or Monastir. The marina at Hammamet is aimed at a more up-market clientele than the other two. Sidi Bou Said has also been used.

Hauling for the winter has usually been in one of the marinas at Sidi Bou Said, El Kantaoui or Monastir although other fishing harbour yards have also been used.

Airports

Flights from Tunis to Europe are all year around but these are fairly expensive. In the summer there are charter flights to Monastir and Jerba. Air Malta also operates scheduled flights to Tunisia. One other alternative to flying you can consider is crossing from Trapani (Sicily) or Genoa by ferry.

Shoestring cruising

The relatively cheap cost of living ashore, and cruising the coast, has meant Tunisia is a popular option for shoestring cruisers. Many of the harbours do not charge yachts and marina charges are around the charge band 2/3 mark. The only bugbear is the expense of getting in or out of Tunisia if you are leaving the boat there.

Reading

RCC North Africa, Van Rijn/Graham Hutt, Imray.
Imray Mediterranean Almanac, edited by Rod Heikell, Imray.

ALGERIA

For many years there has been a bloody civil war between the FIS and the Algerian government. In recent years things have calmed down somewhat, but Algeria is still not on the cruisers' wish list and if you are contemplating visiting here you should check the Foreign Office website for the latest situation.

Reading

RCC North Africa, Hans Van Rijn/ Graham Hutt, Imray.

MOROCCO

The Mediterranean coast of Morocco is bordered for the most part by the Rif mountains. The coast runs from Algeria up to the Strait of Gibraltar where North Africa is around 8 miles away from Europe. Along the Moroccan coast there are two Spanish enclaves at Ceuta and Melilla. Much of the cruising around Morocco is from Gibraltar or Spanish marinas a short distance away on the European side. There are good yacht harbours at Melilla, Kabila, Marina Smir and Ceuta.

Weather and seasons

The climate is a mix of North African and Mediterranean with very hot dry summers and mild winters. At times Atlantic weather systems will affect the climate and it may rain or be foggy. Winds are predominantly from the west or east at the Atlantic end of the coast, going to west towards Algeria. There are frequently days of calm in the summer.

Formalities

Yachts must clear in and out of every harbour. Usually the harbour officials will arrive at your boat and Customs may want to search it. At times your passport will be kept and a shore pass issued. In the future, things may change as Morocco sees more yachts visiting its shores.

Ashore

Even in quite small villages you will find basic provisions and other goods. In larger villages and towns there will be a market with fruit and vegetables, bread, herbs and spices etc. In Ceuta there are good supermarkets with a wide range of foods at low prices.

Eating out in Morocco varies from up-market French/international cuisine in cities and tourist areas (including marina projects) and more humble eateries in the back streets or on the outskirts of town. Personally I nearly always go for the latter but, generally, eating out in Morocco is relatively cheap. The cuisine varies from tourist-type fare, grilled meat and fish with chips, to typically North African dishes like *couscous* and *tajines*. There is also good local fast food like the *brik* (pancake with filling).

Yacht facilities

The only travel hoist is at Marina Smir where there are also some repair facilities. Alternatively, Spanish marinas with hoists and hardstanding are a short distance away on the European side of the Mediterranean.

For wintering afloat, really only Marina Smir and Ceuta are used. Most yachts head for Spain or Gibraltar.

Fishing boats in the harbour in Agadir, Morocco.

Shoestring cruising

Harbour and marina charges are relatively low and ashore the cost of living is very cheap if you are careful. The only problem with cruising along the Moroccan coast is that it is difficult to anchor, or use very small harbours, without the authorities becoming suspicious that you are smuggling either *kif* or people. In some cases yacht skippers have been arrested just for anchoring, so either inform the authorities of your intention to anchor somewhere or, in practice, give up the idea and go to main harbours.

Reading

RCC North Africa, Van Rijn/Graham Hutt, Imray.
Imray Mediterranean Almanac, edited by Rod Heikell, Imray.

Appendix 1
Checklists

TOOL KIT AND SPARES

The following list is the basic kit you should have for a longish cruise. While most tools can be bought in most of the countries around the Mediterranean, the odds are that you will need a tool that you don't have when you are nowhere near a town to buy it. Make adequate provision for stowage of the tools. Most boats have two tool kits: a small one for everyday use with pliers, mole-grips, screwdrivers, adjustable spanner, insulation tape, shackle-key, old knife, WD40, and any other bits and pieces commonly used; and the heavy duty tool kit, which need not be instantly accessible. Stow the heavy duty tool kit in a dry place so the tools don't get rusty; if necessary wrap them in oily rags.

Engine
- Complete socket set, metric or imperial depending on your engine
- Set of open and/or ring spanners (metric or imperial)
- Large adjustable spanner (big enough for the propeller nut and seacocks)
- Medium and small adjustable spanners
- Set of Allen keys
- Set of screwdrivers

Additional tools
- Torque wrench
- Adjustable filter clamp
- Puller

General
Some of the above will be used for general purposes as well, but you will also need:
- Medium and small mole-grips – probably the most-used tool on board
- Medium and small pliers
- Pipe wrench
- Claw hammer and small tack hammer
- Steel tape measure
- Medium wood saw and padsaw
- Hacksaw and spare blades
- Stanley knife
- Medium wood chisel
- Surform
- Flat and ratstail file
- Hand drill or rechargeable electric drill and set of drill bits

Wotchamacallits
- Insulation tape and self-amalgamating rubber tape
- PTFE tape
- Assorted cable ties
- Selection of stainless steel jubilee clips
- Selection of stainless steel wood screws and selftappers
- WD40 and multipurpose lubricating oil
- Sealing spray for electrics – waterproof grease
- Silicone sealant
- Assorted split pins and stainless steel seizing wire
- Lengths of single and double core electrical wire
- Seizing line and assorted cordage

- Bungee cord
- Bulldog grips
- Assorted conical wooden plugs
- Two part epoxy glue (Araldite) and general one tube adhesive
- Gasket goo and contact adhesive
- Rubber gasket material or old inner tube
- Shackles of all shapes and sizes
- Polyester resin and gelcoat, glass cloth and mat
- Safety goggles, dust masks, and thick plumber's gloves

Engine spares
Minimum engine supplies:
- Engine and gearbox oil
- Appropriate greases (winch, general purpose, etc)
- WD40 or equivalent
- Gasket goo (for emergency gasket repairs)

Minimum engine spares:
- Oil and fuel filters
- Head gasket and top-end gasket set if possible
- Impellers for raw water pump (change annually)
- Pulley belts
- Injector sealing washers and O-ring kit (as required)

If possible add:
- Spare injector or nozzle
- Injector liner and washers
- Water pump spares kit
- Thermostat

Other spares
- Dinghy repair kit
- Toilet overhaul kit or at least gaskets
- Galley and bilge pump overhaul kits or at least spare gaskets

- Spare gas regulator and rubber gas tubing
- Sail repair kit – sail repair tape is essential for 'get-you-home' repairs
- Spare block(s)

MEDICAL KIT

Your first requirement is a good first aid handbook. *Ship Captain's Medical Guide* HMSO, *First Aid at Sea* by Douglas Justins & Colin Berry, Adlard Coles Nautical and *A Traveller's Guide to Health* by Lt Col James Adam are all good. The manuals should be put somewhere readily accessible. The first aid kit should contain *at least* the following:

- Sterilised lint and bandage packs
- Sterile burn dressings
- Adhesive dressing (a roll of non-water-proof tape and individual waterproof dressings)
- Cotton wool
- Disinfectant (Dettol)
- Antiseptic (Savlon, TCP)
- Mild painkiller (Aspirin, Veganin)
- Anti-histamine cream (for insect bites and stings)
- Calamine lotion (burns and rashes)
- Diarrhoea treatment (Kaolin and morphine, Lomotil, Enterosan)
- Wide spectrum antibiotic (Amoxycillin, Tetracycline)
- Anti-seasickness tablets (Stugeron)
- Tweezers and scissors

The above is the most basic kit you should take. In addition I would seriously suggest you add the following:

- Suture strips (instead of stiches for wounds)
- Antibiotic ear drops (for local ear infections from swimming)
- Antibiotic powder (for infected wounds)
- Eye drops
- An aerosol burn treatment (Burneze)
- An aerosol sting treatment (Waspeze)

Most of these items can be obtained over the counter or on prescription from a doctor once you explain what you are doing. In the Med, many of these items (antibiotics, anti-histamines) can be obtained over the counter without a doctor's prescription. You should check out any allergies that you or your crew might have to classified dangerous drugs before you leave.

Appendix 2
Useful Reading and Websites

History and pre-history

The Mediterranean and the Mediterranean World in the Age of Phillip II (vol I & II), Fernand Braudel, Fontana. Appears ponderous but is fascinating reading.

Mankind and Mother Earth Arnold Toynbee, Paladin. Readable history of the Mediterranean.

Ulysses Found Ernle Bradford, Century Hutchinson.

The Mediterranean: Portrait of a Sea Ernle Bradford.

The Ulysses' Voyage and The Jason Voyage Tim Severin, Hutchinson.

The Prehistory of the Mediterranean D H Trump, Penguin.

The Garden of Eden David Attenborough, BBC Publications.

Weather

Heaven's Breath Lyall Watson, Coronet.

Instant Weather Forecasting Alan Watts, Adlard Coles Nautical.

On board

Mediterranean Cruising Handbook Rod Heikell, Imray.

Mediterranean Almanac ed Rod Heikell & Lucinda Heikell, Imray.

Coastal Navigation Gerry Smith, Adlard Coles Nautical.

The Practical Pilot Leonard Eyges, International Marine.

The Boatowner's Mechanical and Electrical Manual Nigel Calder, Adlard Coles Nautical.

Yachtsman's 10 Language Dictionary Barbara Webb & Michael Manton, Adlard Coles Nautical.

First Aid at Sea Douglas Justins & Colin Berry, Adlard Coles Nautical.

Ocean Passages and Landfalls Rod Heikell & Andy O'Grady, Imray.

Natural history

The Natural History of the Mediterranean Tegwyn Harris, Pelham.

Hamlyn Guide to the Flora and Fauna of the Mediterranean Hamlyn.

Flowers of the Mediterranean Anthony Huxley & Oleg Polunin.

Cuisine

Mediterranean Cookbook Arabella Boxer, Penguin.

Mediterranean Seafood Alan Davidson, Penguin.

A Book of Mediterranean Food Elizabeth David, Penguin.

Food in History Reay Tannahill, Paladin.

Book websites

www.adlardcoles.com; www.imray.com; www.bookharbour.com

Yachting organisations websites

Royal Yachting Association: www.rya.org.uk

Cruising Association: www.cruising.org.uk

Maritime and Coastguard Agency: for yacht registration, SOLAS regs etc. www.mcga.gov.uk

Radio communication agency: www.ofcom.org.uk/radiocomms/

Other websites

Foreign Office: go to Travel Advice for latest information on visiting countries: www.fco.gov.uk

EasyJet: www.easyjet.com

Ryanair: www.ryanair.com

Flybe: www.flybe.com

Western Mediterranean distance tables

Ajaccio	Alghero	Algiers	Alicante	Barcelona	Bizerte	Bonifacio	Cagliari	Calvi	Cartagena	Formentera	Gibraltar	Ibiza	Mahon	Malaga	Marina Smir	Marseille	Mellila	Oran	Palma	Port Camargue	Port Vendres	Propriano	Sète	Tangier	Tarragona	Toulon	Valencia
96																											
408	336																										
481	431	198																									
299	284	281	231																								
302	221	337	503	439																							
44	84	399	493	316	261																						
213	141	324	463	364	124	172																					
54	139	441	496	305	348	89	259																				
525	471	203	61	281	526	527	499	552																			
391	343	146	94	171	423	396	377	419	138																		
756	703	414	295	517	749	762	726	781	239	363																	
382	333	153	101	161	417	387	369	409	148	12	379																
239	191	198	249	147	308	242	239	265	291	160	514	151															
704	651	364	244	464	690	707	669	733	191	319	63	327	471														
761	707	416	301	518	749	763	726	789	247	376	26	383	526	74													
181	216	411	402	189	428	209	333	167	457	331	689	321	214	636	694												
679	621	309	224	444	638	681	628	704	169	297	136	306	444	115	129	619											
578	514	199	159	365	526	577	521	607	116	208	237	218	426	195	232	537	148										
332	281	171	166	132	376	536	326	364	214	78	447	70	102	394	451	288	372	281									
229	256	408	384	166	468	258	382	217	437	313	673	303	222	619	674	57	601	521	274								
255	264	351	321	91	447	280	368	252	373	252	606	243	174	553	609	111	534	458	209	76							
24	91	403	483	305	293	31	205	71	524	391	758	391	239	704	761	197	677	575	333	241	265						
243	269	404	371	151	466	272	383	231	423	302	655	292	217	606	549	74	586	508	261	21	59	254					
783	728	436	321	541	774	784	745	806	266	393	31	403	547	88	38	713	157	254	471	697	631	781	681				
345	325	276	192	49	471	561	398	345	245	149	477	140	168	424	481	236	406	336	129	213	149	349	198	503			
147	189	406	414	201	408	181	318	133	469	339	703	330	214	649	704	41	628	543	296	88	134	161	106	722	247		
439	406	229	96	163	501	450	452	456	148	93	382	108	229	329	387	347	311	241	141	326	259	442	309	407	121	359	

Central Mediterranean distance tables

Argostoli	Benghazi	Bizerte	Cagliari	Catania	Corfu	Crotone	Derna (Libya)	Kalamata	Khania	Kithira	Levkas	Monastir	Otranto	Pantelleria	Patras	Pilos	Reggio Calabria	Sfax	Siracusa	Tobruk	Trapani	Tripoli (Tarabulus Gharb)	Valetta	Zakinthos
373																								
534	594																							
576	687	124																						
265	406	307	369																					
103	458	558	589	282																				
172	443	441	451	145	160																			
349	153	692	768	741	439	468																		
136	314	611	681	364	224	291	259																	
247	302	701	771	476	321	396	204	134																
181	283	643	701	391	268	335	207	74	62															
71	412	561	579	279	61	171	381	166	267	207														
497	511	143	238	276	529	399	617	564	248	593	518													
158	491	506	537	234	84	98	489	286	388	327	132	489												
429	493	113	198	208	462	331	584	501	592	538	452	89	421											
69	393	591	627	321	126	229	361	148	248	186	67	553	197	482										
101	304	583	628	319	187	254	258	43	147	85	127	532	249	472	106									
246	424	315	324	49	262	123	475	341	441	396	256	311	213	246	303	303								
528	498	222	308	314	567	436	616	592	662	618	554	93	526	151	596	557	351							
261	380	290	391	29	289	157	447	334	436	377	281	248	247	181	316	309	69	287						
411	231	782	846	549	501	537	85	311	243	250	438	701	553	667	419	314	550	692	526					
418	526	133	176	211	427	288	599	506	595	549	418	161	376	77	466	465	166	226	194	679				
583	354	337	431	304	537	419	482	508	566	524	513	213	509	246	528	486	341	168	276	569	311			
323	358	249	329	111	361	234	447	386	466	413	346	184	322	139	377	354	148	222	83	527	171	195		
36	451	551	597	289	126	198	316	103	207	141	65	506	184	441	52	65	267	552	284	376	431	486	338	

Index